Ripley's Believe It or Not!

SPECIAL EDITION 2010

3-D LENTICULAR COVER

SCHOLASTIC INC.

New York   Toronto   London   Auckland   Sydney
Mexico City   New Delhi   Hong Kong   Buenos Aires

ISBN-13: 978-0-545-14345-5
ISBN-10: 0-545-14345-4

PUBLISHING

Developed and produced by Miles Kelly Publishing Ltd
in association with Ripley Publishing

Publishing Director: Anne Marshall
Art Director: Sam South
Managing Editor: Becky Miles

Project Editor: Rosie Alexander
Picture Researcher: James Proud
Editorial Assistant: Amy Harrison
Designer: Rocket Design
Indexer: Hilary Bird
Reprographics: Stephan Davis

12 11 10 9 8 7 6 5 4 3 2 1   9 10 11 12 13 14/0

Printed in China
First printing, September 2009

CONTENTS

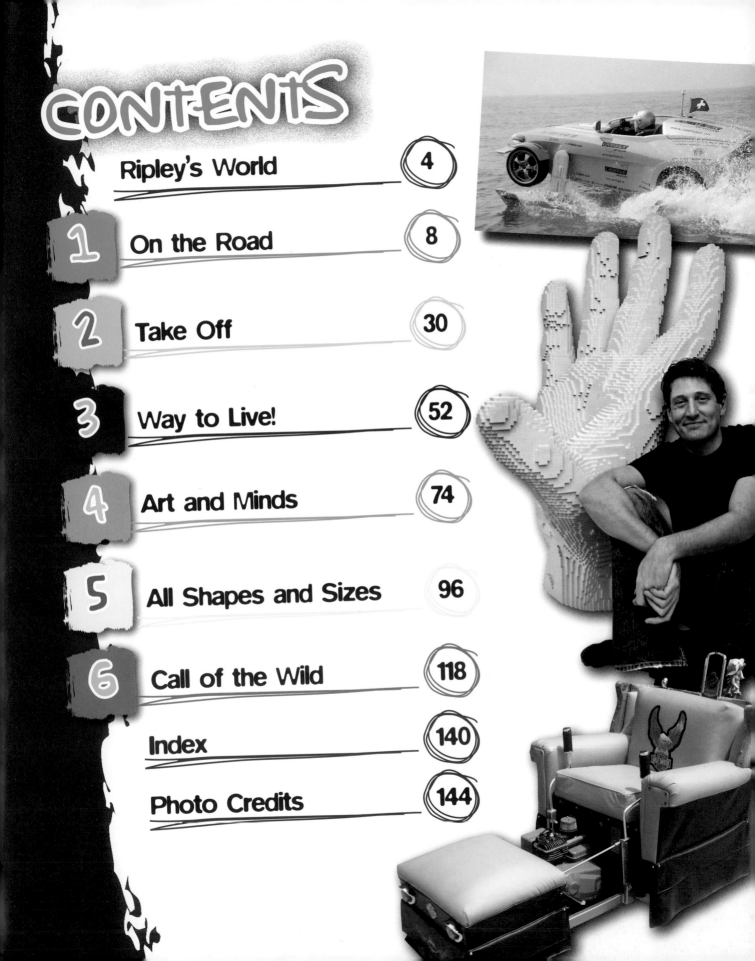

RIPLEY'S WORLD

At the heart of the new Ripley's Believe It or Not! museum in London is a life-size, talking hologram of Robert Ripley. Safari hat on, pen in hand ready to draw at a draughtsman's desk, he looks the man he was: a great explorer, a careful recorder of the variety of human life on our planet, and a figure of huge energy and style.

It was in 1918, while Ripley was working as an illustrator for the *New York Globe* that he began recording the quirky wonders of the world in a cartoon column called *Believe It or Not!* So popular were his illustrations that a pile of 3,500 letters landed on his desk every day, each one from a different fan supplying him with information for his column.

The immaculately dressed Ripley became a true celebrity of his time, tirelessly traveling—he visited 201 countries and covered a total of 464,000 miles—as he scoured the globe for amazing stories.

Although he died in 1949, the artifacts he collected on his travels are on display in the 30 Ripley's Believe It or Not! museums (or Odditoriums) around the world. Ripley researchers still comb the globe for more crazy creations and freaky feats to add to the massive collection.

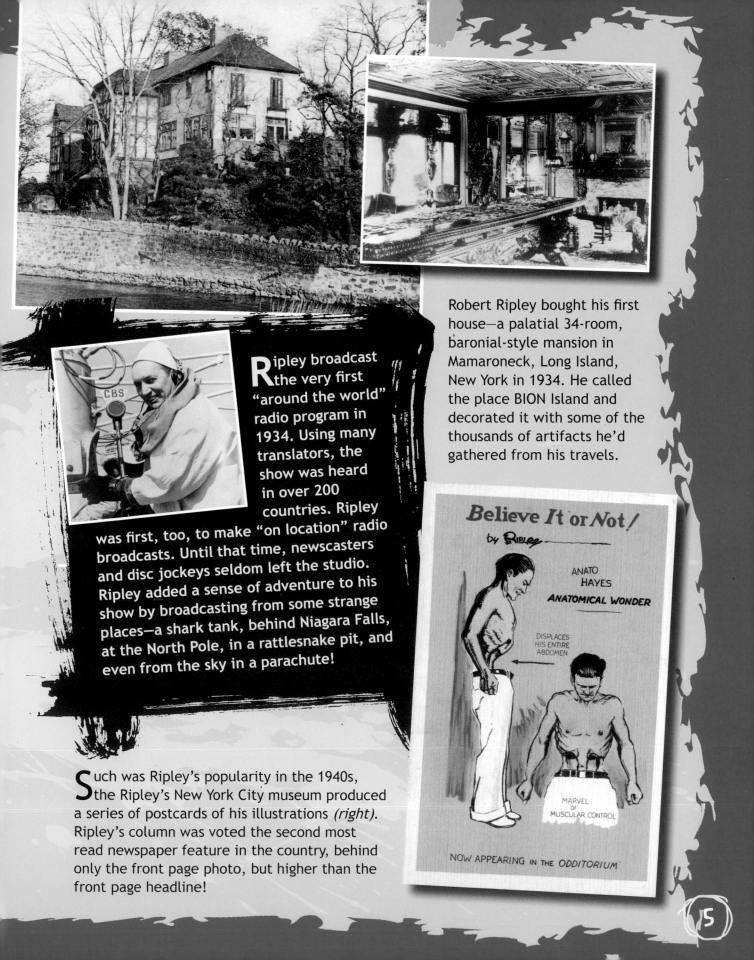

Robert Ripley bought his first house—a palatial 34-room, baronial-style mansion in Mamaroneck, Long Island, New York in 1934. He called the place BION Island and decorated it with some of the thousands of artifacts he'd gathered from his travels.

Ripley broadcast the very first "around the world" radio program in 1934. Using many translators, the show was heard in over 200 countries. Ripley was first, too, to make "on location" radio broadcasts. Until that time, newscasters and disc jockeys seldom left the studio. Ripley added a sense of adventure to his show by broadcasting from some strange places—a shark tank, behind Niagara Falls, at the North Pole, in a rattlesnake pit, and even from the sky in a parachute!

Such was Ripley's popularity in the 1940s, the Ripley's New York City museum produced a series of postcards of his illustrations *(right)*. Ripley's column was voted the second most read newspaper feature in the country, behind only the front page photo, but higher than the front page headline!

Believe It or Not!
by Ripley

ANATO HAYES
ANATOMICAL WONDER

DISPLACES HIS ENTIRE ABDOMEN

MARVEL OF MUSCULAR CONTROL

NOW APPEARING IN THE *ODDITORIUM*

"This old world is a mighty interesting place"

…wrote Robert Ripley, and just one glance at this book is enough to prove his point. Spin the compass and go north to spy cricket being played at the North Pole; head south and find Chile's craze for dressing dogs in fancy costumes; be amazed in the west by a 122-foot snow woman; and in the east join in with some human-sized foosball.

Ripley also said that...

"the truth is stranger than fiction"

...and nothing in this book is untrue. Believe It or Not, there *is* someone who lives on a tropical island made from recycled plastic bottles. There *is* a boat built from bricks (it floats!), and a couple who invited a bison to their wedding. Get ready for a freefalling haircut at 14,000 feet, and try on for size some new slippers with headlights—so you'll never go bump in the night!

The black-and-white photographs in this book are taken straight from the Ripley's Archive. Some even may have been taken by Ripley himself. He reproduced the images as cartoons in his newspaper column.

RIPLEY'S ★ ARCHIVE ★

GLANCE AT THE TICKER RUNNING ALONG THE BOTTOM OF EACH AND EVERY PAGE...

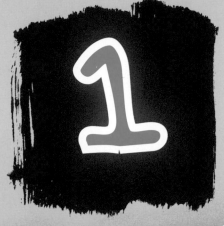

1

ON THE ROAD

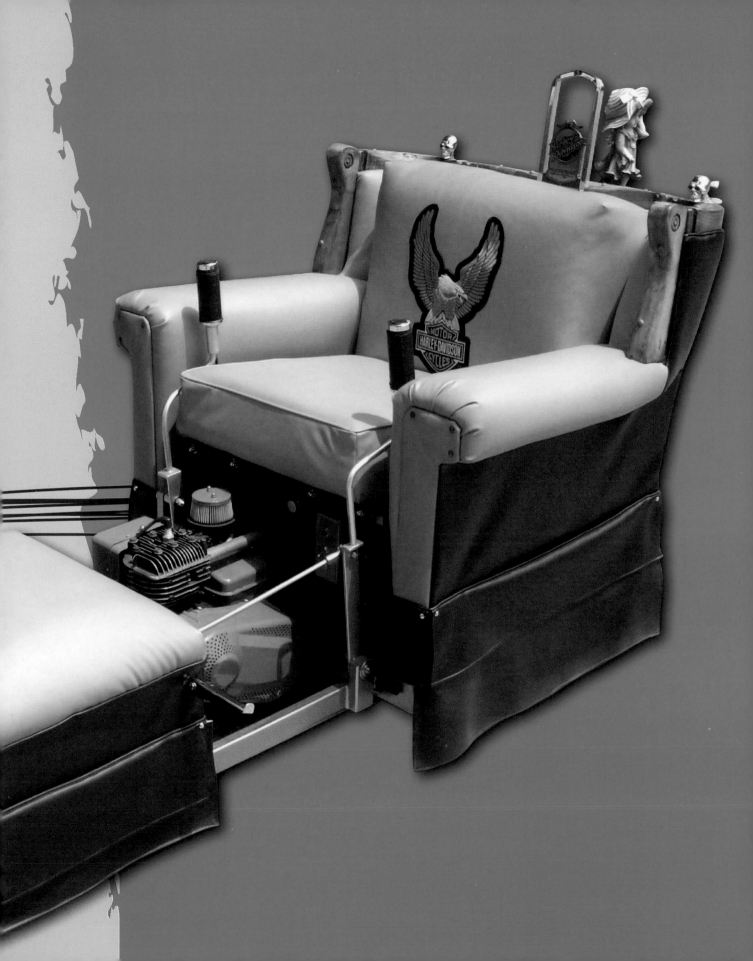

PICK A MOTOR

Car Car

UK artist James Ford's tribute to the *Dukes of Hazzard* car, General Lee, began with the purchase of a 1981 Ford Capri. Posing as a toyshop owner, he then bought 2,000 toy cars at a trade fair, but needed another 2,300. An appeal brought donations from around the world. Contributors were encouraged to leave a message in, or on, their cars, and three years later the car-covered car, named General Carbuncle, was complete.

Double Vision

If you see this car coming towards you on the highway, don't panic! You may think the upside-down car will topple over at any minute, but it is perfectly roadworthy. The creation of Dennis Clay from Houston, Texas, this mirror image effect is made by welding together two identical VW Beetles. It may look bizarre, but it could have a practical advantage if you break down. Why stop at carrying just a spare tire?

★ INSPIRED BY THOMAS STEVENS, WHO PEDALED AROUND THE WORLD ON A PENNY FARTHING IN

Crystal Cruiser

Embellished with more than one million Swarovski crystals in 50 colors to represent the 50 U.S. states, Ken and Annie Burkitt's American Icon car was commissioned to promote a range of greeting cards. It took four artists six months to place the stones on the 2006 Mini Cooper, which is now worth more than a million dollars. The husband-and-wife design team's other crystal-encrusted artworks include a 12-string guitar, a carousel horse, and a model of a human skull.

Plane Speaking

The largest plane flying today is the Russian Antonov 225, originally designed to carry the Soviet space shuttle, with a wingspan of 290 feet. The passenger airliner Airbus 380 has a wingspan of 258.86 feet and a fuselage the length of two blue whales. The biggest plane ever built was Howard Hughes's wooden flying boat, the "Spruce Goose," which had a wingspan of 320 feet. It made just one flight on November 2, 1947.

1884, JOFF SOMMERFIELD FIRST PLANNED HIS OWN WORLD TOUR IN 1998. FOUR PENNY FARTHINGS

SET YOUR SIGHTS

Catch a Wave

Where would you find a wave in the middle of the desert? Sculpted by wind and water, The Wave, a spectacular rock formation south of the Utah/Arizona border, was once a field of Jurassic sand dunes—perhaps home to Stegosaurus and Allosaurus. The soft sandstone is so fragile that the number of visitors is restricted to 20 a day—ten chosen from an online lottery and ten picked using bingo balls at the entrance to the trail.

Flaky Fortune

Illinois

A good knowledge of geography helped two sisters from Virginia earn $1,350 from the sale of a single frosted cornflake. Fifteen-year-old Emily McIntire was munching on cereal when she spotted a flake that resembled the state of Illinois. Her sister, Melissa, suggested they auction the Prairie State-shaped flake on eBay, where it was bought by Monty Kerr of Trivia Mania, from Austin, Texas. He decided to pick up the flake in person after a previous purchase, supposedly the world's largest flake, broke into pieces while in transit.

AND SEVERAL BROKEN BONES LATER, SOMMERFIELD FINALLY LEFT LONDON IN MARCH 2006.

Seeing Red

This photo has not been retouched. The bright orange-red soil of this Chinese landscape is called laterite. It forms in tropical parts of the world where high rainfall washes away the water-soluble metals in the clay leaving a concentration of iron, which is responsible for the strange color. As you might expect, this brick-red clay makes good bricks—South-East Asian temples built of laterite have been standing for more than 1,000 years.

Snow Joke

It looks like the world's largest frosted donut, and at over two feet tall it's way too big for dunking. This rare phenomenon, spotted in the North Cascades, Washington State, is known as a snow donut and starts out as a giant snowball, called a snow roller. Snow rollers form when chunks of snow are blown along by the wind or roll down a slope, gathering extra snow. The centers are weak and can be blown away, leaving a donut shape.

THE TRIP HAS TAKEN HIM ACROSS EUROPE, AUSTRALIA, NEW ZEALAND, ASIA, THE U.S., AND

TRAVELING IN STYLE

Just asking...

Who are Doug and Heath?
Doug is an L.A. web geek. Heath, who taught English in Korea, now works in London.

Why the tuxedos?
"What better way to attempt to say 'It doesn't matter what you look like' than to wear tuxes and hang about until people take notice? And nobody's ever going to take us seriously dressing like backpackers are they?"

What were the rules of the trip?
"Tuxedos must be worn for a minimum of twelve hours a day. Clothes can be added or removed, but the outfit should always be recognizable as a tuxedo."

What reactions did you get to your attire?
"People thought we were going to a marriage, or that we were Western businessmen, professional snooker players, magicians, or just complete nuts."

Soon after meeting in Hong Kong, Doug Campbell and Heath Buck planned a journey to London. This was to be a trip with a twist— the pair would wear tuxedos throughout the 6,000-mile trek! Their mission was to raise money while helping local people along the way, and their charitable deeds included plowing in Vietnam, working with tuberculosis patients, and painting a monastery in Tibet. Having survived temperatures between 120°F and well below freezing as they traveled through 19 countries, the well-dressed duo arrived in London on August 18, 2007—170 days after setting off.

CANADA. BY OCTOBER 2008, HE HAD TRAVELED 21,155 MILES, RAISING $28,150 FOR CHARITY.

Grow As You Go

Is this the ultimate in green motoring or the perfect picnic spot? The Chinese turf-top was on display at the 2008 Beijing Flower Show to promote the latest in soil-free growing technology. New York performance artist Gene Pool took the green theme to extremes in 1997 with his grass-covered bus, complete with a matching living-grass uniform of suit, hat, and shoes. Both the bus and the outfit had to be watered daily.

Relaxing Roadster

It may not be street-legal, but an Armchair Cruiser is the ride of choice for the speed freak with a taste for soft furnishings. This gasoline-powered Harley Davidson model can reach a top speed of 40 miles per hour and perform wheelies. Or riders can choose the electric version for a quieter, more relaxing drive. Handcrafted by a family firm in Indiana, the Cruiser has feather-soft cushions, is driven using a joystick, and comes with optional stereo system, drinks cooler, and "bling package."

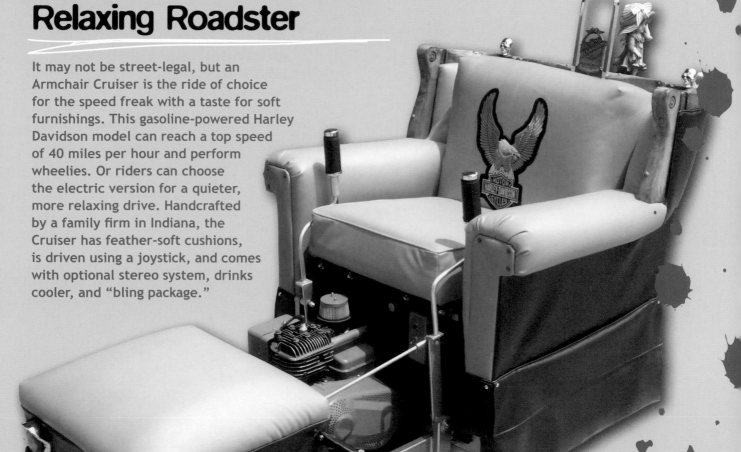

★ THE WORLD'S HIGHEST RAILROAD RUNS ACROSS CHINA FROM BEIJING TO LHASA, TIBET—

WACKY TOURISTS

Teddy Tourists

Teddy bears in need of a vacation should head for Germany, where "teddy tour" operators will show them the sights. Hundreds of bears from around the world have made the trip, some arriving with snacks and headache pills, others with pocket money for ice cream. Special activities such as bungee jumping, golf, or fishing can be arranged and, at the end of their one-week stay, toys are shipped back to their owners with a photo album recording their adventures.

Trunks in Lobby

An elephant never lets much get between itself and its food. Mfuwe Lodge, in Zambia, has been built on the path one herd takes to reach a certain mango tree. When the tree ripened one year and the elephants returned, the herd continued to take the path they had always taken—even when it meant passing through the hotel's lobby. Now the family strolls through up to four times a day.

THE WORLD'S LOFTIEST CAPITAL CITY. MOST OF THE TWO-AND-A-HALF-DAY JOURNEY IS AT

Little Londoners

Watch where you put your feet in London, because you might tread on one of street artist Slinkachu's Little People. Slinkachu hand-paints the one-inch-tall figures and places them in everyday situations—from sight-seeing near Big Ben, or reading on the subway, to sitting on a park bench. It takes about four hours to install and photograph the models, which is tricky on London's busy streets. The artist was once questioned by a police officer who queried the time Slinkachu was hanging around as he set his characters in place.

New Age

Julius Brittlebank of Charleston, South Carolina, lived for 14 days more than his age. How did he do it? Brittlebank made 14 round-the-world trips, each time traveling from east to west. Every time he crossed the international date line, which runs along the 180° line of longitude in the middle of the Pacific Ocean, he gained an extra day.

RIPLEY'S ARCHIVE

ALTITUDES ABOVE 13,123 FEET, REACHING 16,640 FEET AT THE HIGHEST POINT, SO THE AIR

NEIGHBORHOOD WATCH

In Stitches

There's something about this house that reminds visitors of the gingerbread cottage in the story of *Hansel and Gretel*. In fact, it's a 140-square-foot house knitted by hundreds of women across the world. The brainchild of Alison Murray from Bideford, England, its outside walls are covered with fuzzy sweets and Popsicles. Inside, visitors can perch at a table for afternoon tea.

Moving Story

This 750-year-old, 660-ton church in Heuersdorf, Germany, was sitting on mining land and had to be moved 7½ miles to more secure ground. Such drastic action is occurring increasingly around the world. How is it done? Expert House Movers in the U.S. say they move a building by first digging under it. They then insert four feet of steel beneath the structure before raising everything six feet onto a wagon. Only if the wagon crosses soft ground does the building start sliding!

IN THE SEALED CABINS IS ENRICHED WITH OXYGEN AND EACH SEAT HAS ITS OWN OXYGEN

Builder with Bottle

Did you know that Americans drink 13.15 billion gallons of carbonated drinks a year? Statistics like that must delight Maria Ponce who constructed her entire house in El Borbollon, El Salvador, out of empty plastic bottles. She even made an intricate mosaic floor out of all the bottle tops.

Body Building

Walk through an open wound in the leg of the 115-foot-tall man sitting on the Corpus building in Oegstgeest, Holland, and enter a human body museum. Inside this huge figure the fiberglass body parts are giant-sized. You feel tiny as you climb into a vast nose and experience a sneeze, or bounce on a rubber tongue while being deafened by a burp.

TOP SPEEDS

Chair-raiser

Giuseppe Cannela of Bedfordshire, England, successfully attached a jet engine to the back of his mother-in-law's wheelchair to reach speeds in excess of 60 miles per hour.

Up and Away

Australia's Matt Mingay really only needs one wheel on his motorbike. In March 2005, at Temora Aerodrome, New South Wales, he reached a speed of 140 miles per hour doing a motorbike wheelie over a distance of 0.6 miles.

Feeling Flush

In 1999, Hank Harp drove a motorized toilet 874 miles—the length of Britain. Perched on the toilet seat, Hank stored supplies he needed for the trip in the bowl and drove at four miles per hour.

Fair Play

Max Tate of Newcastle, England, has converted a fairground bumper car into a vehicle capable of 90 miles per hour.

Shopping Shock

The shopping cart adapted and motorized by Edd China can hit speeds of 60 miles per hour. China, from Maidenhead, Berkshire, England, who has previously built a motorized sofa, shed, and four-poster bed, spent six months designing the cart, which is over 11 feet tall, nearly ten feet long, and six feet wide. It is powered by a 600cc motorbike engine hidden in a huge shopping bag, its driver sitting in an oversized child seat.

Blind Ambition

In 2006, in the French Alps, Kevin Alderton, a former soldier from England, set a downhill skiing speed record for blind people, reaching 100 miles per hour.

INTO THE GROUND TO ENSURE IT STAYS FROZEN DURING THE SUMMER MONTHS TO KEEP THE RAIL

Race at a Pace

Never has the milk-cart been so fast-track as when Welsh racing-driver Richard Rozhon took the wheel. He managed to get the humble electric machine to reach 73 miles per hour at a milk-cart speed trial in Leicestershire, England, in 2003.

Board Out of His Mind

Billy Copeland rode his rocket-powered skateboard at an amazing 70 miles per hour, the fastest skateboard speed ever recorded. Worryingly, when he made this piece of skating history, he didn't have any brakes. Instead, he strapped a scrap of tire onto his running shoe and slammed his shoe down at the end of his run.

Climb Time

Most climbers take around four days to reach the summit of Mount Everest from Base Camp, but in May 2003, Sherpa Lhakpa Gelu made the ascent in just under 11 hours, beating the previous best time—also held by a Sherpa—by nearly two hours.

Super Stool

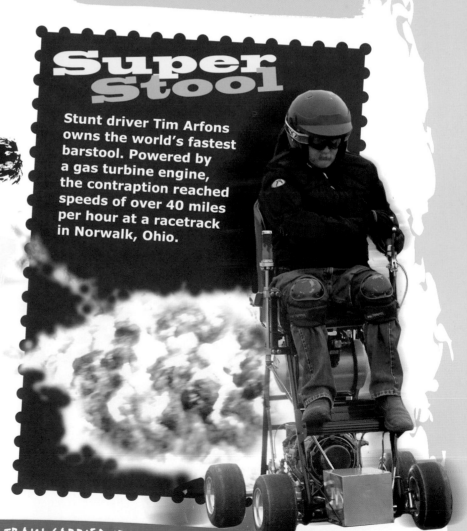

Stunt driver Tim Arfons owns the world's fastest barstool. Powered by a gas turbine engine, the contraption reached speeds of over 40 miles per hour at a racetrack in Norwalk, Ohio.

Remote Control

Imagine hurtling at speeds of up to 168.4 miles per hour—in total darkness. That's the experience of blind rider Mike Newman from Manchester, England, who has raced on a 1,000cc motorbike, guided only by radio instructions.

BE PREPARED

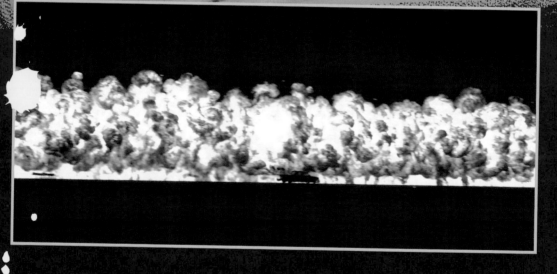

More powerhouse than an outhouse, Paul Stender's Port-O-Jet is powered by a 50-year-old, 750-pound Boeing jet turbine, bought for $5,000. The former NASCAR and Indy car mechanic from Indiana was inspired to build the wheeled washroom when he saw a windstorm blow portable toilets across the tarmac. During his shows, Stender shoots 30-foot fireballs from the burner before making a high-speed run at up to 46 miles per hour. The outhouse is piloted from the original toilet seat.

WESTERN AUSTRALIA ON JUNE 21, 2001. IT MEASURED 4.568 MILES AND HAD 682 CARS PULLED

Bucket Business

Cell phones, laptops, and Wi-Fi mean it's possible to work just about anywhere these days. But some people can take the mobile office concept one step further with the Office In A Bucket (OIAB). Looking like a cross between an igloo and a bouncy castle, the OIAB inflates in just eight minutes. This mobile office is great as a hideaway for open-plan office workers who don't see eye-to-eye with their colleagues.

Commuter Coat

Falling asleep on public transportation can be a pain in the neck. Matthew Gale from San Francisco has invented the "Excubo" (Latin for *I sleep outside*)—a coat for tired travelers. The huge collar can be turned up to support a snoozer's head and prevent dozers from drooling on their neighbors.

Seeker Sneaker

New York inventor Isaac Daniel has combined a pair of sneakers with a GPS chip that can locate the shoes anywhere in the world. The idea isn't to track down your lost sneakers when you're about to rush out the door, though. These special shoes have been designed to find children, hikers, military personnel, and elderly people if they get lost. The panic button will alert the law enforcement agency. The shoes are expensive, but can be a lifesaver.

HEAD FOR THE SEA

Incredible Edibles

When English photographer Carl Warner creates his dramatic panoramas, his first stop is the refrigerator. A closer look at this seascape reveals that it is composed entirely of food. Carrot stalactites hang from rye-bread rocks, while cauliflower, broccoli, exotic fruit, and pasta make up the underwater scene. Other "foodscapes" show peas hanging like fruit from broccoli trees surrounded by potato rocks, and a pea-pod boat floating on a smoked-salmon sea. It takes Warner three days to complete each colorful landscape.

Aussie Aquanaut

When marine biologist Lloyd Godson won the *Australian Geographic* "Live your dream" Wildest Adventure Competition, people were surprised to learn that his dream was to spend two weeks sealed in a six-foot-tall box 15 feet underwater. The BioSUB project aimed to prove that it was possible to create a self-sustaining environment relying on plants to produce oxygen and absorb carbon dioxide. Godson survived by cultivating algae watered with his urine. He used a pedal-powered generator and solar panels to supply electricity to his laptop, and enjoyed his days responding to e-mails and playing his drum kit.

MARATHON EVERY WEEKEND FOR THE WHOLE OF 2006 TO RAISE MONEY FOR CHARITY. DANE

Bigger Splash

Interested in a few laps at the pool? Think twice if you're staying at Chile's luxurious San Alfonso del Mar resort. At more than 1,000 yards long with an area of 20 acres and a 115-foot deep end, this massive man-made, saltwater lagoon holds 66 million gallons of water—equivalent to 6,000 standard pools. It took five years to build and cost almost two billion dollars. The maintenance bill alone comes in at four million dollars a year.

Way to Glow

This eerie blue shimmer, seen in the waters of the Marlin Marina in Cairns, Australia, is caused by millions of glow-in-the-dark plankton. Known as bioluminescence, the phenomenon is a light-producing chemical reaction, similar to that of a glowstick. The plankton glow when the water is disturbed, probably as a defense mechanism to dazzle predators. During 1918, a German submarine was destroyed in the Mediterranean after glowing plankton revealed its position.

WATCH OUT

It's a Gas

As fuel prices rise, free gas might seem to be a dream come true. But when methane gas started erupting from the ground in Shandong village, Chongqing, China, it caused buildings to crack and created holes in the ground up to ten feet wide. The village had been built above a coal mine, which produced the natural gas that seeped into people's homes. To avoid being poisoned, villagers set fire to the escaping gas, before being evacuated to safety.

Hot Property

When it comes to property, location is everything. So building a house in the shadow of the world's most active volcano may not be a wise investment. Kilauea in Hawaii has been erupting continuously since 1983, spewing out enough lava each day to fill almost 300 Olympic swimming pools. But Jean Olson says there is no place she would rather be. She and other lava-loving residents enjoy the spectacular views, which draw thousands of visitors each day. At a temperature of more than 2,100°F, the lava incinerates or buries everything in its path.

Outback Oddball

James Stirton was cycling around his cattle farm
in the Australian outback when he came across an
odd-shaped ball of shredded metal. A curator from
the Brisbane Planetarium concluded that it was a
tank from a rocket used to launch two satellites
from Cape Canaveral, Florida, in 2006. Thousands
of pieces of space junk fall to Earth each year, but
the chance of being hit is estimated at less than one
in a trillion, compared to a one in 1.4 million risk of
being struck by lightning.

★ Going Green ★

An area of western Siberia, Russia,
has come under the spotlight as
scientists predict that thawing
permafrost, covering an area
the size of France and Germany,
could double the amount of
methane in the atmosphere and
increase global warming by ten to
25 percent. This barren plain is
the world's largest peat bog and
contains a quarter of all methane
stored on Earth—some 70 billion
tons, which has been trapped in
the frozen soil until now.

Watch This Space

Mega Mountain
The largest known volcanic mountain in the Solar System is Olympus Mons, on the planet Mars. It is 372 miles across and 15 miles high. The tallest mountain on Earth, Mount Everest, is only 5½ miles high.

Rare Event
If something happens "once in a blue Moon," it occurs about 15 times every 20 years. What we call a "blue Moon" is the second of two full Moons in one month—a rare event.

Nothing to It
Although it is nine times as big as the Earth, the planet Saturn would actually float in water if you had a big enough pool. This is because of its incredibly low density.

Intergalactic Power
The engine that drives a space shuttle is as powerful as 39 train engines, yet that engine is only $\frac{1}{7}$ of the weight of a train's engine. In 25 seconds, the shuttle's engine can pump enough fuel to fill a swimming pool, and the overall power of a space shuttle at takeoff is equivalent to 16 million horsepower. Despite this, the humble flea can accelerate about 50 times faster, relative to its size.

Hot Star
A pinhead-sized speck of the burning gases from our sun could kill a man from 99 miles away.

Paper Plane Experiment
If you threw a paper plane in space, it would float away in the same direction forever because there is little or no gravity in outer space. It would continue until it hit an object. If you did the same inside a spaceship, there would still be no gravity, but the air required for breathing would lift the wings so that the plane flew upward. Back on Earth, Tony Fletch of Wisconsin managed to fly a paper plane 193 feet—almost the length of a jumbo jet.

Lightning Lava
Volcanoes on Jupiter's moon can spew out hot material at speeds of 0.6 miles per hour. That is 20 times faster than the average volcano on Earth.

PIECES OF PURE GOLD IN ITS LAVA. ★ VULCAN ISLAND, PAPUA NEW GUINEA, ROSE FROM THE

Mixed Veg
In space, if a frozen pea floated into a cloud made of cola, it would explode.

Hot at North Pole
Earth's North and South poles are moving. Some think that they are shifting faster because of an increased use of electricity in our homes. It's predicted that, in about 300 years, Earth's magnetic North Pole will be located around Kansas and magnetic South Pole will have moved into the Southern Atlantic Ocean, close to South Africa.

Old Timer
Planet Earth is roughly a third of the age of the universe—about 4.5 billion years old.

Lethal Clothing
In 1965, American astronaut Edward White lost a glove while on a spacewalk from *Gemini IV*. It remained in orbit for a month, reaching speeds of 17,400 miles per hour, and posed a lethal danger to spacecraft until it burned up.

Space Trash
There are thousands of pieces of space junk in orbit around Earth. The oldest manmade debris that is still hurtling around our planet is the U.S. satellite *Vanguard I*, which was launched 50 years ago, in 1958.

Dirty Solar System
The Mir space station threw more than 200 rubbish bags into space over ten years. They are all still in orbit to this day.

King of a World
The planet Uranus, discovered in 1781, was originally known as "George's Star" after King George III of England.

Orbiting Egg
Despite what people may think, the Moon is not actually round. It is the shape of an egg. When you look at it in the sky, you are looking at one of the "ends." This is because, the gravity of Earth pulled the Moon toward the planet when it was formed.

Dangerous Debris
When a Pegasus rocket exploded in space in 1996, the debris was estimated to be 300,000 fragments. The Hubble Space Telescope was twice as likely to be hit by space debris after this incident.

OCEAN FLOOR IN ONE NIGHT IN 1870. THE VOLCANO QUICKLY GREW INTO A 600-FOOT PEAK.

2

TAKE OFF

TESTING TASKS

Pool Prodigy

When two-year-old Korbyn Horomona started swimming lessons, her coach quickly realized she had a special talent and predicted that she would be able to swim 1,000 yards by the age of three. The coach was right—Korbyn achieved her 1,000-yard goal, using a mix of freestyle and backstroke. But she didn't stop there, Korbyn just turned around and kept on swimming until she had completed an astonishing 1,750 yards, or almost a mile. It took the Australian toddler an hour and a half to swim further than most kids her age would be able to walk.

Speedy Scot

Scottish cyclist Mark Beaumont became the fastest man to ride around the world, when he crossed the finishing line at the Arc de Triomphe in Paris 195 days after setting out. Smashing the previous record by 81 days, he pedaled 18,297 miles and traveled through 20 countries. He suffered food poisoning in Pakistan, was knocked off his bike three times (by a donkey, a motorbike, and a car), was robbed in Louisiana, and had to ride through torrential rains and fierce headwinds, but he says he never felt like giving up.

★ WHEN A GNOME DISAPPEARED FROM THE GLOUCESTER, UK, GARDEN OF EVE AND DERRICK

Hair-Raising Cut

We all know that you're not supposed to run with scissors, and nowadays you're not even allowed to take them on a plane. But it seems that no one told Israeli hairdresser Oren Orkobi. Having already completed an underwater haircut, Orkobi took hairstyling to the opposite extreme and cut the hair of diving instructor, Sharon Har Noy, while skydiving 14,000 feet above Habonim beach, Israel. Orkobi had one minute to complete the haircut.

Jogging Giant

Lloyd Scott "ran" the 2008 London Marathon dressed as a nine-foot-tall robot. Based on the character from the movie *The Iron Giant*, the 70-pound costume had stilts in the legs, a moving mouth, and eyes that lit up. Scott, a leukemia survivor, has raised more than £5 million (about $9 million) for cancer research and other charities. The former London firefighter crossed the finish line six days after setting off—two days faster than in 2006, when he took part wearing a suit of armor weighing 100 pounds and dragging a 200-pound dragon.

Extreme Feats

★ Stefan Minten from Bonn, Germany, is a professional stair climber, or skyscraper runner. His record for running to the top of the Empire State Building is 16.34 minutes. The total length of the stairs he has scaled is greater than the distance from the Earth to the Moon.

★ Michal Kapral of Toronto, Canada, completed the 26-mile Toronto Waterfront Marathon in just two hours 50 minutes nine seconds, juggling three beanbags. He took two minutes off the previous "joggling" record.

★ The music of J.S. Bach echoed through a long Swiss automobile tunnel when violin-maker Christian Adam of Lübeck, Germany, decided to try playing the violin while cycling—backward. It took Adam five hours eight minutes to ride 37½ miles perched on the handlebars with a music stand fixed to his saddle.

★ Colorado real estate agent Don Claps performed 1,293 cartwheels in one hour on a live TV show.

STUART-KELSO, THE COUPLE ASSUMED HE HAD BEEN STOLEN BY STUDENTS. SOME MONTHS LATER,

WAY TO GO

High Flier

David Smith Sr. found a novel way to beat the lines at the Mexican border. The human cannonball was launched headfirst over the rusty fence between San Diego, California, and Tijuana, Mexico, landing in a net on the Mexican beach. Smith had special permission to cross the border this bizarre way, but he carried his passport, which he waved as he flew through the air. The one-time math teacher has been fired from a cannon around 9,000 times without breaking a single bone and has raised a high-flying family—his son, two daughters, and a cousin are all human projectiles.

Motoring Mystery

How could "Texas Zeke" Shumway from Dallas, Texas, drive cars and motorcycles more than 50,000 miles but never get more than 25 feet from his starting point? The answer is that he set off from the center of a 46-foot-wide motordrome and drove round and round the track. Motordromes were popular during the 1920s and early 1930s. The tracks banked up to 60 degrees, creating high G-forces on drivers. Spectators watching from above were at great risk if a car lost control. After a number of accidents involving fans and drivers, motordromes were gradually replaced by dirt tracks.

HOWEVER, THE GNOME REAPPEARED ON THEIR DOORSTEP, LOOKING A LITTLE THE WORSE FOR

Soaring Centenarian

While most centenarians in the UK are happy with a card from the Queen, this British great-grandmother chose to mark her hundredth birthday in a more exciting way by paragliding from the top of the Five Finger Mountains in Cyprus. Peggy McAlpine, who did a bungee jump at the age of 80, leaped from the 2,500-foot peak and enjoyed a 15-minute tandem flight before sharing a bottle of Champagne with her family. Currently the world's oldest paraglider, she is hoping to repeat the experience when she reaches 105.

Rocket Roller

At first, professional inline skater Dirk Auer was more interested in distance than speed, spending several weeks skating through Spain, then nonstop from Frankfurt to Munich, Germany, in less than 24 hours. Then he turned his talents to more extreme stunts, including skating down a roller coaster while holding a glass of water and straight down the wall of a high-rise building. The German daredevil reaches unbelievable speeds. With a jet pack strapped to his back, he zoomed 117 miles per hour through a tunnel in the city of Darmstadt, Germany. In 2007, strapped to three jet engines, he took on an Aston Martin V8 Vantage Roadster in a half-mile race on the British TV show *Top Gear*—sadly, he lost.

WEAR AND STANDING NEXT TO A TIGHTLY WRAPPED PARCEL. THE MYSTERIOUS PACKAGE REVEALED

THINKING BIG

Joshua Taylor doesn't have to go shopping for a Halloween costume. He just needs to choose from his collection of more than 400 masks. Nine-year-old Joshua, from West Jefferson, North Carolina, has been mad about masks since he was a toddler. When he was younger his favorite movie was *The Haunted Mask* and he began wearing a werewolf mask at every opportunity. He even started making his own masks using sliced sausage and tortillas, as well as the more common material papier-mâché, before being given a rubber-mask-making kit for Christmas. Since then, Joshua has come up with an extraordinary range of designs, and his family is planning to make him a basement workshop so he can indulge his talent to the full. Joshua's creepy collection features all kinds of monsters, ghouls, werewolves, skeletons, and aliens—along with the occasional superhero. Anyone who breaks into his house could be in for a fright.

A LEATHER-BOUND PHOTO ALBUM CONTAINING 48 PHOTOS OF THE GNOME ON A WORLD TOUR.

Sole Obsession

Darlene Flynn takes calls on a phone that looks like a red stiletto, eats off plates decorated with shoes, and reads by a shoe-shaped lamp. In fact, almost everything in her house in Romoland, California, resembles or is decorated with a shoe, but the major part of her collection can be found in the display cases that line her living room. Here, more than 700 tiny shoes jostle for space with shoe thimbles and other shoe-themed curios. Darlene has spent around $200,000 on the 7,765 items of shoe memorabilia. But one of her favorite pieces was a Christmas gift from her son—a shoe made of coins worth $15.07 that he spent 40 hours gluing together.

Flush with Success

As a plumber, Barney Smith must have seen a few toilet seats during his working life. Now that he's retired, his garage museum in San Antonio, Texas, is lined from floor to ceiling with hundreds of them. It all started 30 years ago, when he glued a set of deer antlers to a toilet seat lid. Now his collection features license plates, Boy Scout badges, Pokémon cards, false teeth—even a small piece of wreckage from the *Challenger* space shuttle. The one thing he doesn't have is a functioning toilet seat—the museum has no bathroom.

HIS ADVENTURES INCLUDED RAPPELLING DOWN A MOUNTAIN, STANDING IN A SHARK'S MOUTH,

ON A MISSION

Trash in Paradise

In 1998, British eco-pioneer Richart Sowa began building his own paradise island in the sea near Puerto Aventuras, off the coast of Mexico. He filled nets with more than 300,000 discarded plastic bottles, which supported a bamboo framework covered with plywood, and topped it with sand gathered from a nearby beach. Mangroves were planted on the raft—which is 66 x 54 feet—to provide shade. Their roots grew down into the sea and helped to stabilize and anchor the structure. He built a house with a composting toilet, a solar oven, and a plastic-sheeting roof to gather rainwater. Other trees and vegetables were planted to provide food. Chickens, a duck, cats, and a dog joined the lone inhabitant. Sadly, Spiral Island, as it was called, was destroyed by Hurricane Emily in 2005, but Sowa has now built an even better island, Spiral Island II. The new structure, which is 60 feet in diameter and has beaches, a house, two ponds, a solar-powered waterfall, and solar panels, is in a lagoon away from bad weather at Isla Mujeres, Mexico. Volunteers helped on the project, which is still a work in progress, always growing.

Toothpick Triumph

This Ferris wheel and bridge were built entirely from toothpicks by 14-year-old Barry Pariser—27,000 toothpicks were used to construct the wheel alone. Barry built toothpick towers too, but probably not as large as those in Toothpick City, created by Stan Munro. Featuring replicas of some of the tallest buildings in the world, including Taipei 101 in Taiwan, the Petronas Towers in Malaysia, Dubai's Burj Al Arab hotel, and the Washington Monument, this extraordinary sculpture uses more than two million toothpicks.

Marathon Masterpiece

Diagnosed with Cushing's Syndrome as a child, Londoner Annette Banks was not expected to live past her 20th birthday. Because she was interested in history and had a passion for sewing, her father suggested that she recreate the 230-foot-long Bayeux Tapestry, which depicts the 1066 Norman invasion of England. Luckily, Annette's health improved and she married and had children. She kept working on the tapestry and when her father died she vowed to finish it. It took her 20 years, but her 50-foot-long recreation is finally complete. Embroidered on the tapestry are the words: "Dedicated to my wonderful father who has always given me inspiration."

HIC RESIDET: WILLELM: REX·

25ᵗʰ DECEMBER 1066. HERE SITS WILLIAM L KING OF ENGLAND.

THE PE WITH

Towering Achievement

Thousands of visitors to the LEGOLAND® theme park in England have helped build a record-breaking tower. It took four days of hard work and almost half a million bricks to complete the tower, which stands almost 100 feet tall. Children built eight-inch sections that were lifted into place by crane, then the final brick was placed by LEGO® engineer, Bo Dahl Knudsen. The tower is designed to look like a Viking longboat mast to mark the opening of the Land of the Vikings attraction and to celebrate LEGO's 50th birthday.

IN NEW ZEALAND. TWENTY-TWO-YEAR-OLD LAW GRADUATE SIMON RANDLES OWNED UP

KEEP AT IT!

In the Dark

In an astonishing feat of endurance, Geoff Smith, from England, spent 150 days buried underground in a coffin in the garden of a pub. He lasted 49 days longer than his mother; she pulled the same stunt 30 years before.

Foot Feat

Arulanantham Suresh Joachim balanced on one foot for 76 hours and 40 minutes at Vihara Maha Devi Park Stadium, Sri Lanka.

Surf's Up!

From May 2004 to July 2005, Flavio Jardim and Diogo Guerreiro traveled 5,045 miles on windsurfers.

Walk Talk

Dave Kunst of the U.S. traveled the entire world on foot between 1970 and 1974, covering 14,450 miles. He took over 20 million steps, wore out 21 pairs of shoes, and started and ended in Minnesota.

Wakeup Call

In 1964, at age 17, Randy Gardner of the U.S. went an unbelievable 264 hours without sleep and without the help of any medication. On the tenth day of the stretch, his doctor reported that Randy still had the coordination to beat him at pinball.

Stroke of Genius

In 2005, Jim Dreyer of Grand Rapids, Michigan, towed a supply dinghy while completing a 60-hour solo swim across Lake Superior. He battled storms, 15-foot swells, and powerful currents that pushed him off course and increased the distance of his swim from 50 miles to 70 miles. His success meant that he had achieved his goal of swimming across all five Great Lakes.

Human Pin Cushion

Body-piercing fan Kam Ma sat for seven hours 55 minutes while being pierced 1,015 times at Sunderland Body Art Festival, Sunderland, England, in March 2006. A feat all the more remarkable given the lack of anesthetic!

TO BORROWING THE GARDEN ORNAMENT AS A TRAVEL COMPANION. HE SAID IT WAS A GREAT

Marathon Effort

A group of Buddhist monks subject themselves to incredible tasks. They are required to complete a marathon 100 nights in a row wearing straw sandals. In the morning they do chores and pray as usual before running through the night again.

Lapping It Up

A strange race occurred in New York City in 1998. The 3,100-mile course consisted of running around and around a Queens school between 6 a.m. and midnight for weeks on end. The leading runners completed around 115 laps of the school each day. The winner, Istvan Sipos, from Hungary, finished the course in 47 days.

Ride of His Life

Life is one long roller-coaster ride for Chicago University lecturer Richard Rodriguez. Since the 1970s, he has been setting roller-coaster records. In 2007, at Blackpool Pleasure Beach in England, he spent 17 consecutive days riding, sleeping, and eating on the Pepsi Max Big One, completing 8,000 rides and 6,500 miles.

Armed Force

In February 1996, Paddy Doyle of Birmingham, England, performed 8,794 one-armed pushups in five hours, using only his right arm. He can also manage 37,350 pushups in a day and 1,500,230 pushups in a year.

Motor Home

Cathie Llewellyn of Wintersville, Ohio, won a new car in 2005 after living in it for 20 days. All contestants in the competition had been allowed a five-minute break every six hours during the challenge, which took place in a shopping mall in Steubenville, Ohio. Cathie's last remaining opponent gave up because she needed to use the bathroom.

Just Deserts

The Baja 1,000 Desert Race takes place every November. It's a famous test of endurance, in which car drivers sometimes complete the very bumpy 1,000-mile course with broken bones after accidents along the way. Ivan "Ironman" Stewart finished the course in just 20 hours in 1998.

ICE-BREAKER, BUT HE SOMETIMES HAD TROUBLE GETTING IT THROUGH CUSTOMS. ★ MICHAEL MAY

THAT'S NOT POSSIBLE!

To the Point

It takes the warrior monks of Shaolin Monastery, in Henan Province, China, the birthplace of kung fu, three to ten years to master the skills of this unique martial art. Imitating the movements of fighting animals, the monks perform extraordinary physical feats as they scale walls, walk over knives, stand on their fingertips, break bricks over each other, and balance their bodies on the tips of spears. Founded in the fifth century, the Buddhist monastery has been destroyed and rebuilt many times.

Feat of Clay

Pioneering potter Peter Lange loves bricks, but the way he uses them might raise an eyebrow. His two-ton, 20-foot-long brick boat, with its corrugated iron sails, made its maiden voyage on April Fool's Day, 2002. The idea came to the New Zealander when he was working inside a kiln and was reminded of sitting under a boat. It took him three months to make the boat using 676 bricks and it made a successful voyage around Auckland harbor. His other unlikely brickworks include bags, teapots, a bumper car, a "paper" plane, and an airbed.

WAS BLINDED AT THE AGE OF THREE BY A FREAK EXPLOSION. HIS SIGHT WAS RESTORED,

Anyone for Tennis?

Tennis stars Roger Federer and Andre Agassi took the sport to new heights during their friendly game on the helipad at Dubai's sail-shaped Burj Al Arab hotel, which is set on a man-made island. The helipad is 692 feet high, with an area of only 496 square yards. They couldn't find any volunteers to act as ballboys, unsurprisingly, and eventually they had to give up after losing all the hotel's tennis balls.

Mower Man

In 1953, Robert Dotzauer of Los Angeles, California, successfully balanced three lawnmowers on his chin, which, with a combined weight of 145 pounds, weighed five pounds more than he did. Comedian Mark Faje also balances lawnmowers on his chin, but only one at a time. The difference is that Mark's lawnmower is motorized—and running.

RIPLEY'S ARCHIVE

THANKS TO STEM-CELL TECHNOLOGY, AFTER 43 YEARS. NOW THE CALIFORNIAN INVENTOR

Great Escapes

Dedicated Digger
Italian nobleman Giacomo Casanova escaped from a lead-lined prison in Venice in 1755 by digging a tunnel under his cell with a piece of iron he found in the jail yard. When he was moved to an adjacent cell, he persuaded his new neighbor to continue the tunnel and they both escaped together.

Cat Snatch
Bamboo, a cat weighing six pounds eight ounces that was owned by Colleen Hamilton of Esquimalt, British Columbia, Canada, survived after being snatched from the back porch by a Great Horned owl. Bamboo limped home 22 hours later. Judging from its injuries, veterinarians concluded that the cat had fallen from a significant height.

Daring Tunnel
Wolfgang Fuchs of Berlin helped more than 100 people escape into West Berlin in the early 1960s. He dug tunnels under the wall for more than 400 feet, including one that began in a bathroom and allowed more than 55 people to escape from East Germany.

Holiday Surprise
A Massachusetts man was getting ready for his Fourth of July cookout when the fireworks started early: a Ford Taurus drove off an elevated parking lot and crashed through the roof of his house. No one was hurt in the freak accident, but guests were surprised to see the car sticking out of the roof when they arrived to begin the celebrations.

Nailing It
Inmates at a jail in Winston-Salem, North Carolina, found freedom after climbing through a ceiling hole they had scooped out with nail clippers. They then used a rope made from jumpsuits to climb down the prison wall. They were caught, and their nail clippers were confiscated.

Unscheduled Departure
Billy the cat was put onto a flight from Phoenix, Arizona, bound for Philadelphia, where he was due to transfer to a connecting international flight. Billy somehow managed to escape from his cage, and ended up stuck in the plane's cargo hold for 19 days. Eventually, the cat was discovered at Manchester Airport, and was finally reunited with his owners.

Python Package
Staff at a post office in Mechernich, Germany, were horrified to see a five-foot albino python escape from a package. The parcel, labeled "Attention—Glass," had been accepted by the staff and put in the back of the office. But then it started to move and the large snake slithered out of the wrapping.

Moving Target

A German driver who was using an airport runway to practice high-speed driving escaped unscathed in 2005 when a plane landed on his roof. The 55-year-old Porsche driver was traveling at more than 100 miles per hour near Bitburg when the bizarre collision occurred.

Skinny Criminal

In 2006, an Australian prisoner managed to squeeze out of his jail cell after losing more than 30 pounds. He had weighed 154 pounds when jailed in 2003, but had slimmed down to only 124 pounds over three years, and was able to escape after chiseling a gap between the bars and the wall.

Great Survivor

Talbot, a six-month-old stray cat, wandered into a car plant at Ryton, England, in 1999 and went to sleep in the body shell of a Peugeot 206 on the assembly line. With the cat still asleep inside, the shell then went into the paint-baking oven at a temperature of 145°F! Amazingly, Talbot survived, although his paw pads were burned off and his fur was singed.

Royal on the Run

England's King Charles II in 1651 made a daring escape from soldiers scouring the countryside for him. He hid in an oak tree, then in a priest's hideaway, before making his way to France dressed as a lady's maid.

Bid for Freedom

Juan, an Andean spectacled bear, made a dramatic bid for freedom at Germany's Berlin Zoo in August 2004. First he paddled across a moat using a log as a raft, then scaled the wall of his enclosure. Bizarrely, he looked to complete his getaway on a bicycle. Before he could climb onto the bike, he was cornered by zookeepers and immobilized with a tranquilizer dart.

Hot Canadian

Steve Santini is known as "The World's Most Extreme Escape Artist." His "Cremation Chamber" stunt, performed live on TV, involved being handcuffed and padlocked to a chain inside a metal vault, which was heated with flame throwers to 400°F. One of the cuffs jammed and Santini had to hold his breath to avoid the burning air until he could escape.

Tight Spot

World-renowned escape artist David Straitjacket, from Manchester, England, made a dramatic escape from the bottom of a Chinese lake. David was tied with three pairs of handcuffs, 22 pounds of chains, and two padlocks, and had no safety divers.

SPOTLIGHT

IN THE MOUNTAINS WHERE HE BROKE THE RECORD FOR DOWNHILL SKIING BY A BLIND PERSON.

OUT OF THE DARK

Just asking...

What is echolocation?
Dolphins, shrews, and most bats and whales use echolocation to navigate and hunt. The animals make sounds, then wait to hear its echo. The length of time between the sound and the echo shows how far away an object is. The slight time difference before the echo reaches each of the animal's ears indicates direction. Dolphins have especially sensitive echolocation systems and can tell the difference between similar objects, even in a noisy environment.

"I'm not blind, I just can't see," says Ben Underwood, who lost his eyes to cancer at the age of three. As Ben zips around fearlessly on his Rollerblades, rides a bike, and plays football and basketball, the only sign that he is not just an average Californian teenager is the constant clicking sounds he makes. Aged five, Ben discovered that he could find his way around by making noises with his tongue. Now he "sees" with his ears, using echolocation, just like bats and dolphins. Echoes can give detailed information about the size and location of objects, and the type of sound gives further clues—a sharp echo indicates glass, for example. By putting all the information together, Ben is able to build up a picture of his environment. Scientists have discovered that the part of the brain that processes visual images does not stop working when people lose their sight and it can be activated by other senses, such as touch or hearing. One of the earliest known cases of human echolocation is that of British naval lieutenant James Holman (1786-1857), who traveled the world on his own, using the sound of a tapping cane to get around, after losing his sight at 25.

HOWEVER, HE HAS TROUBLE RECOGNIZING HIS FAMILY'S FACES AND EVEN FINDS IT DIFFICULT

Blind Ambition

Miles Hilton-Barber lost his sight in his twenties, but it hasn't stopped him from seeking out challenging adventures. Now in his late fifties, Hilton-Barber, from Derbyshire, England, has hauled a sled more than 250 miles across Antarctica, completed the 150-mile Marathon des Sables across the Sahara Desert, raced the 11-day Ultra-Marathon across China, climbed Mount Kilimanjaro and Mont Blanc, performed more than 40 skydives, and piloted a micro-light from London, England, to Sydney, Australia—a journey of 13,360-miles—with a sighted co-pilot.

Loud Colors

Neil Harbisson always painted in black and white because that was all he saw. The British artist suffers from achromatopsia, or complete color blindness. Then he met cybernetics expert Adam Montandon, who came to lecture at his art college. Montandon decided to try to solve Neil's disability and invented the Eyeborg, a system that converts the way in which colors reflect light at different frequencies (with violet light vibrating the fastest and red the slowest) into sound. Now Neil can "hear" 360 colors.

Seeing Is Believing

★ Dominic Head, of London, was born with such weak eyelids he had to tip his head backward to see. Doctors took a strip of tendon from his thigh and used it to link his eyelids with his forehead muscle to allow him to open his eyes.

★ Although he has a co-pilot in case of emergencies, blind pilot Steve Cunningham, from Banbury, England, takes full control of his plane, using talking computer software that updates him on its height, position, and speed.

★ After giving birth to her first baby, British mother Mandy Rotchell, who was partially blinded after suffering from glaucoma, was warned that she might lose her sight entirely if she had any more children. Now the proud mother of nine is legally blind but has never regretted giving up her sight for her large family.

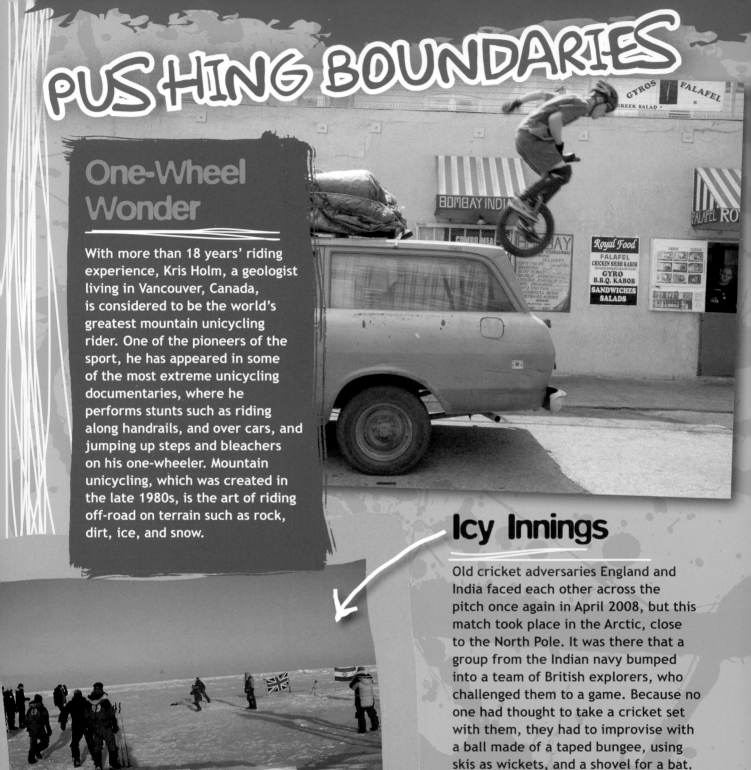

PUSHING BOUNDARIES

One-Wheel Wonder

With more than 18 years' riding experience, Kris Holm, a geologist living in Vancouver, Canada, is considered to be the world's greatest mountain unicycling rider. One of the pioneers of the sport, he has appeared in some of the most extreme unicycling documentaries, where he performs stunts such as riding along handrails, and over cars, and jumping up steps and bleachers on his one-wheeler. Mountain unicycling, which was created in the late 1980s, is the art of riding off-road on terrain such as rock, dirt, ice, and snow.

Icy Innings

Old cricket adversaries England and India faced each other across the pitch once again in April 2008, but this match took place in the Arctic, close to the North Pole. It was there that a group from the Indian navy bumped into a team of British explorers, who challenged them to a game. Because no one had thought to take a cricket set with them, they had to improvise with a ball made of a taped bungee, using skis as wickets, and a shovel for a bat. Cricket was not the only game played during the expedition. One of the British team was a member of the English Bridge Union, and together they played bridge at the North Pole on an ice table.

SKIING WAS MUCH EASIER BEFORE HE REGAINED HIS SIGHT, BECAUSE HE FINDS THE NEW VISUAL

Fearless Fishermen

The Khon Phapheng waterfall in southern Laos is the biggest in Southeast Asia. During the rainy season a huge volume of water roars over the falls from the Mekong River, which is rich in fish. Local fishermen take great risks tightrope-walking above the jagged rocks and white water so they can fish among the rapids.

Aerial Antics

★ British couple Darren McWalters and Katie Hodgson exchanged their wedding vows while standing on the wings of two biplanes 1,000 feet above the ground. The minister flew ahead on a third aircraft.

★ Twice a year, people in southern China and Southeast Asia climb flimsy bamboo ladders 200 feet above the ground to collect the nests of cave-dwelling swifts for birds' nest soup, risking certain death if they fall.

★ Leaving his plane behind, Swiss pilot Yves Rossy flew for nearly six minutes thousands of feet above the Alps with an eight-foot jet-powered wing strapped to his back. Using the same method in 2008, he crossed the English Channel in under ten minutes.

The Lionwhisperer

Animal behaviorist Kevin Richardson, who is based at a wildlife conservation area near Johannesburg, South Africa, has such a bond with big cats that he can play-fight with lions and is happy to kiss, cuddle, and spend the night curled up with them. He claims he can make friends with any lion less than a year old, because it is still young enough to accept him as part of its family. However, Richardson once had a close call when an aggressive four-year-old male started biting him. Fortunately, Richardson's quick decision to display passive behavior stopped the lion in its tracks.

WHY WOULD YOU DO THAT?

Cannonball Catcher

Pain-proof fitness instructor Ken Richmond has a stomach of steel. His shows of strength include having a wrecking ball collide with his belly, having a cannonball dropped on his head, and having a cannonball fired at his stomach. As the cannon prepares to fire, Richmond tenses his belly. When the cannonball hits, he starts to double up and is thrown backward by the impact, falling into the straw bales behind him.

Stretch Your Legs

Austrian Jewgenij Kuschnow held a side-split position between two stationary cars for an impressive 36.48 seconds during the Impossibility Challenge in Dachau, Germany, on March 30, 2008. This annual event attracts competitors with all kinds of unusual talents, such as juggling with a ball and two chain saws, tearing up telephone directories, making tiny paper ships, and nonstop laughing.

Hold on Tight

Called "Game for brave people," this eye-wateringly high swing has been set up on the 700-foot-high viewing platform of a TV tower in Heilongjiang Province, China. The swing takes people beyond the platform's edge, over the city of Harbin. At 1,100 feet, the tower is the world's second highest steel tower, after the Kiev tower in Ukraine.

Ready for a Bite?

Georges Christen from Luxembourg started bending nails as a teenager. Soon he turned his attention to tearing a deck of playing cards, then telephone directories. His next tools were his teeth. In 1987, he used them to stop a fully revved 110-horsepower Cessna plane from taking off, then, using both arms and his teeth, he held back three Cessnas. In 1991, he pulled a 100-ton ship 100 yards upstream. Later he turned a 65-ton,150-foot-high Ferris wheel with his teeth. On one occasion, Christen bit into a table and carried it with his teeth—while someone sat on top.

HE KEPT JUMPING EVEN AFTER FRACTURING HIS WRIST. HE NEEDED 15 PARACHUTE PACKERS TO HELP.

3
WAY TO LIVE!

HOME IS WHERE THE ART IS

Dream Screens

TV sets are not normally huggable, but this cute blue elephant is just asking for a squeeze. Choose from a zooful of animal designs including a zebra, a giraffe, and a monkey. If cuddling the TV is not your thing, there are fire trucks, big rigs, and steam locomotives, too. The TV in the shape of a box of fries with a ketchup packet remote could have you reaching for the phone to order a burger. For a healthier option, try the apple, complete with leaves and a stalk.

★ GIANT VEGETABLES FROM SPACE COULD SOLVE THE PROBLEM OF FEEDING CHINA'S 1.3 BILLION

Find the Person

Australian artist Emma Hack had her first taste of body art as a teenager, painting children's faces at parties for pocket money. After studying makeup artistry at college, she was inspired to create her 3-D "living wallpaper." The process is exhausting for both artist and model because it can take up to 19 hours to painstakingly copy the patterns onto the model's body. Hack sometimes includes animals in her wallpaper works and has recently started painting on cows and horses, too.

Pencil Palace

The three-story stairwell of Jaina Davis's San Francisco home is plastered with pencils. Jaina says she's always loved office supplies, so she was happy to go along with mosaic artist Jason Mecier when he suggested taking the pencil theme to extremes. The project, which used 92,626 pencils, took five years to complete and cost $50,000. The designs include a futuristic pencil portrait of Jaina when she reaches her 80s, a compass cactus forest, wind chimes made of rulers, and a built-in notepad.

Water Wheels

The road doesn't stop at the sea for this ultra-light concept car. At the push of a button, the Rinspeed Splash transforms into an amphibious vehicle, and an integrated hydrofoil system enables the Splash to "fly" two feet above the water. Powered by a 750cc natural-gas engine, the vehicle reaches speeds up to 125 miles per hour as a sports car, 30 miles per hour as a boat, and 50 miles per hour as a hydrofoil. The bodywork is made of a state-of-the-art plastic normally reserved for Formula One racing cars.

THE EARTH FOR TWO WEEKS, BEFORE RETURNING TO BE CULTIVATED IN HUGE HOTHOUSES. THE

Truck Transformer

Brazilian Olisio da Silva and his two sons, 28-year-old Marcus and 20-year-old Marco, have created a real-life Transformer. Accompanied by loud music, smoke, and flashing lights, the body of their ordinary-looking Kia Besta van rears up and, six minutes later, it has morphed into a 12-foot robot. It took the da Silva family from São Paulo nine months and $122,000 to create the "SuperRoboCar."

Fly Drive

Jim and Chris Milner's AirCar might get you out of a jam. At the flick of a switch, the car unfolds its giant wings to reveal a pair of propeller engines. Jim Milner, a former pilot, always dreamed of building a flying car. His son, Chris, an engineer based in Bethesda, Maryland, hopes to turn the dream into a reality. On the road the vehicle will reach a top speed of 85 miles per hour; in the air it will cruise at 200 miles per hour at 25,000 feet. The AirCar could be on sale by 2010.

438·RNJ

HUNGRY TO WIN

Just asking...

How did you start competitive eating?
"I eat more than normal people, so I thought it might be something I'd be good at. I won a qualifier for the annual July Fourth contest three years ago at Nathan's Famous Hog Dogs on Coney Island, New York. In the final, I ate 25 hotdogs with buns in 12 minutes—a new women's record."

You are only five feet five inches with a tiny frame—have you got an unusual digestive system?
"Most top eaters are not heavy—skinny people have less fat to restrict the stomach. You need a large throat, or esophagus, to get the food down, a strong jaw for chewy foods, and a big stomach capacity. Mine holds 18 to 20 pounds of food."

Do you feel ill after a contest?
"No—an average contest consumption will only be about nine pounds of food in ten or 12 minutes—that's not enough to fill me up!"

Korean-born Sonya Thomas is ranked among the top ten competitive eaters in the world, yet she weighs less than 100 pounds. Regularly "out-eating" men three times her size, Thomas, who now lives in Alexandria, Virginia, considers her particular specialties to be seafood and hard-boiled eggs because of her nimble fingers. Her eating records include 11 pounds of cheesecake in nine minutes, 80 chicken nuggets in five minutes, 65 hard-boiled eggs in six minutes 40 seconds, 46-dozen oysters in ten minutes, and 44 lobsters in 12 minutes. Competitive eating began at country fairs in the early 20th century and now has its own federation, the IFOCE, to regulate the increasing number of contests around the world.

Delectable Dress

It is supposed to be unlucky for the groom to see the bride in her wedding gown before the ceremony, but Valentyn Shtefano didn't just see the dress, he made the dress. Shtefano is not a dress designer as you might expect, but a Ukrainian baker. He whipped up his wife Viktoriya's gown using caramel and 1,500 cream puffs. Viktoriya had to wear the dress, which eventually weighed in at 20 pounds, every night for two months while her husband-to-be attached the cream puffs. He also made her tiara, bouquet, and necklace from caramelized sugar.

Sausage Sundae

Perhaps inspired by innovative English chef Heston Blumenthal's famous bacon-and-egg ice cream, traditional British food company Aunt Bessie's has come up with a savory alternative to the classic cone. Aunt Bessie's customized ice cream van, rechristened the "Mash Van," will sell cones filled with mashed potato topped with a hot sausage, gravy, and peas instead of the usual chocolate chip or raspberry ripple.

RADIATION, MICRO-GRAVITY, OR MAGNETIC FIELDS WERE RESPONSIBLE FOR CREATING THE

ON THE MENU

Baby-Faced Spud

We know that potatoes have eyes, but when Mr. Feng of Heilongjiang Province, China, was given this large tuber by a rural relative, he spotted a nose and a mouth too—and soon realized that it looked just like a baby's face.

Weird Watermelon

This strange-looking fruit is not genetically modified. It is produced by placing a box around the melon so that as it grows it fills the surrounding shape. Space-saving cuboid melons first went on sale in Japan several years ago and sell for a massive $82 each. Chinese growers took the technique one step further by producing square melons embossed with Olympic mascots to mark the 2008 games. Compared to the Japanese fruits, they are a bargain at just $52 each.

HUGE VEGETABLES. ★ WHILE MOST PEOPLE ENJOY FOOD COOKED OVER CHARCOAL, 78-YEAR-OLD

Eccentric Eateries

Customers at a restaurant in Wuhan, capital of Hubei Province, China, are unlikely to run off without paying. Qiufan, which means *inmate's restaurant*, is a prison-themed steakhouse where handcuffs hang on the walls and diners sit inside cells divided by iron bars. At D.S. Music Restaurant in Taipei, Taiwan, guests sit around a hospital bed and are served by waitresses dressed as nurses. Crutches decorate the walls, and visitors are greeted by a wheelchair in the lobby.

Giant D'oh-Nut

Weighing the same as two rhinoceroses, this giant donut was created in Sydney, Australia, to celebrate the DVD release of *The Simpsons Movie*. It took 40 people more than nine hours to build the 20-foot-wide sugary sculpture, using over 90,000 donuts, half a ton of pink icing, and 66 pounds of sprinkles. The donuts were later donated to a charity that collects food for disadvantaged people.

ZHENG RONG-SHI LIKES TO EAT THE WARM COAL ITSELF. THE WIDOW FROM GUANGDONG PROVINCE,

WHAT A LIFE

2's Company

In 2002, computer-game fan Dan Holmes officially changed his name to Mr. PlayStation 2. Holmes, from Banbury, England, played for four hours a day and had previously asked a few ministers to marry him to his console. "None were keen," he said. "So I took its name instead."

How Green You Are

Ever since he was a child, Bob Green has been obsessed with the color from which his last name is derived. He picked his home to suit, living on West Green Street, Greencastle, Indiana, wears green clothes, drives a green car, and even named his three children after various shades of green—Forest, Olive, and Kelly.

Good Gourd

Marvin Johnson and his wife Mary had so many strange-looking gourds at their house in Angier, North Carolina, that they set up a Gourd Museum in 1965. The exhibits are mostly of gourd art. There's a gourd xylophone, a gourd Popeye, and a zoo of gourd animals.

What a Steal

A San Francisco woman who wanted a gas stove for her apartment stole one from a neighboring building—without turning off the gas. She caused a $200,000 explosion.

Bond, Matt Bond

A collector of Agent 007 memorabilia for more than 20 years, Matt Sherman of Gainesville, Florida, has turned his den into a shrine to James Bond, complete with books, jewelry, and even cologne relating to his hero. He turns routine shopping trips into pretend MI6 missions in which his two young children are given assignments to pick up certain grocery items within a specified time. He has also spent more than $10,000 on spy equipment that he uses for monitoring purposes.

Spooky House

Charles and Sandra McKee of Waxahachie, Texas, have spent $250,000 creating a replica of the house from *The Munsters* TV show. Designed from set photos and TV clips, the two-story, 5,825-square-foot house contains secret passages, Grandpa's dungeon, and a trapdoor leading to the quarters of Spot—the McKees' dog, who was named after the fire-breathing dragon that the Munsters kept as a pet.

CHINA, STARTED TO EAT CHARCOAL 30 YEARS AGO FOLLOWING THE DEATH OF HER HUSBAND.

Home Fires Burning

To demonstrate his love for his girlfriend, Hannes Pisek made a huge heart out of 220 burning candles on the floor of his apartment in Hoenigsberg, Austria. Sadly, while he was picking her up from work, his burning heart set fire to the apartment. He not only lost his home but also his girl, who promptly went back to live with her parents.

Dressed Up to the Canines

Dogs in Nunoa, Chile, must have huge closets at home. Their owners have started a trend of dressing their pets in fancy costumes when taking them for a walk. Dogs about town have been seen dressed as Batman and Robin, Easter bunnies, Cinderella, and Snow White. They have even been known to wear tuxedos or wedding dresses!

Look Who's Tolkien

Believe it or not, American *The Lord of the Rings* fan Melissa Duncan is so obsessed with the films that she sits down to dinner with cardboard cutouts of the characters!

Royal Ruse

In 2003, Nick Copeman changed his name officially to H. M. King Nicholas I. Calling himself "Britain's other monarch," he rode on horseback, in full uniform, through Sheringham, Norfolk, sold nobility titles over the Internet, and started the Copeman Empire from his palace—a two-berth motorhome.

Tree's a Crowd

In the jungles of the Brazza River Basin in the Indonesian province of Papua, local tribes have slowly built their way up into the trees to escape pests lurking on the ground. Their homes now reach dizzying heights of over 100 feet.

Sticky Business

Gary Duschl of Virginia shares his home with a ten-mile-long gum-wrapper chain he's spent 40 years creating. It weighs 730 pounds. To travel the length of the chain would take ten minutes in a car traveling at 60 miles per hour.

Stain Pain

A man from Clermont, France, blew up his house when he added gasoline to a washing machine to try to remove a grease stain from his shirt. A spark ignited the gasoline and the first floor of his home, knocking him unconscious.

HANGING OUT

Seniors with Swords

Residents at a retirement home in Melbourne, Australia, are fighting old age through fencing. The senior citizens, who are mostly retired priests and nuns, are studying swordplay to help keep them mobile and sharpen their wits. Sixteen men and women, all aged over 80, cross swords at the weekly classes at the Corpus Christi home.

Full-Size Foosball

Table soccer goes large with this inflatable human football arena, seen here drawing the crowds outside a department store in Hangzhou, eastern China. The players are attached to plastic poles that slide from side to side across the giant field. There are five people on each team, and they are able to move only at the same time as their polemates. Unfortunately, no spinning is possible in this man-sized match.

Iron Head

Skilled kung fu artists are well known for being able to stand on one finger, or stand on their heads without using their hands. But this kung fu fan from Nanjing, China, has chosen to practice his skull stand on top of a bottle. The pressure on his cranium is thought to be 290 pounds per square inch.

Pain in the Neck

A lightweight wife is not necessarily an advantage at the American Wife Carrying Championships, held in October at the Maine resort of Sunday River, because the prize is five times her weight in cash. The sport originated in Finland and there are several techniques—piggyback, fireman's carry, or Estonian-style where the wife hangs with her legs around the husband's shoulders, holding on to his waist. The 278-yard course begins with an uphill run and includes a waist-deep water obstacle.

It Can Only Get Better

Unlucky Number
Sentenced to seven years in jail, a man from San Antonio, Texas, begged the judge not to give him seven years because seven was his unlucky number. So the judge gave him eight years.

Language Barrier
Best of luck to foreigners learning the English language and encountering the 29-letter word "floccinaucinihilipilification," which means "the action of estimating as worthless." It's also tricky to fully understand the word "set," which has close to 200 meanings.

Magic Tree
The acorn was traditionally believed to inspire good fortune, youthfulness, and strength. At the time of the Norman Conquest (1066 CE), the British would carry dried acorns to ward off violence.

Buried Alive
Two reclusive brothers met an undignified end when the elder brother, Langley Collyer, while taking food to his bed-ridden brother, accidentally set off his own booby trap and was buried under a weighted suitcase, a sewing machine, and hundreds of old, stacked newspapers. The brothers were infamous hoarders. Unfortunately, his brother then died of starvation when Langley never arrived with food.

Ice Attack
Large thunderstorms can produce lumps of ice of a frightening size. Hailstones the size of tennis balls devastated the Indian city of Moradabad in 1888, killing more than 240 people. The countries of India and Bangladesh have suffered the most human fatalities by hailstones.

Good Luck Obsession
George Kaminski has a strange obsession. While in prison for a 25-year stretch, he collected 72,927 four-leaf clovers from the prison grounds. He started his collection to show that you can do anything you set your mind to. When he moved to a minimum-security facility in 2005, he was horrified to find that there were no clovers anywhere on the grounds. His great rival collector, Edward Martin Sr. of Soldotna, Alaska, was then able to add to his collection of 76,000 four-leaf clovers unopposed.

Key Facts
The ancient Greeks used a key as a mark of wisdom and good fortune. Traditionally, wearing three keys together represents the keys to wealth, health, and love.

(328 FEET) ON A SINGLE 100-METER-LONG PAIR OF SKIS. ★ A SPA RESORT IN HAKONE, JAPAN,

Super Star

In ancient times, it was believed that good fortunes were decided by the stars, hence the phrase "Lucky Star."

Belly Laughs

In the early 1900s, the Fore Tribe of Eastern New Guinea was discovered to suffer from the "laughing disease" Kuru, so-called because the symptoms include uncontrollable laughter. The illness spread quickly due to the traditional tribal practice of eating their enemies. Fortunately, the disease disappeared along with the practice of cannibalism.

Unlucky 8

American George E. Spillman of Texas was a "number 8" man—he died at 8 p.m. on August 8, 1988, age 88.

Dress Sense

Female members of a southern India tribe, the Toda, wear only two garments in their lifetime, each made from a single piece of cloth. They receive their second robe when they are married, after wearing the first one since childhood.

Hot Hotel

In 1912, the brand-new Howard Hotel in Baltimore was found to have a serious fault—when staff members lit the fireplaces, the smoke couldn't escape because the builders had forgotten to add chimneys.

You Win Some

Dennis L. Wheat, from Malvern, Arkansas, won his car in a raffle. Unluckily for him, he later discovered that it was the same car he had traded in six years earlier!

Crazy Climate

Bogor, a city on the island of Java in Indonesia, lies in an area that produces thousands of thunderstorms each night. The city received an average of 322 days of thunder per year between 1916 and 1919.

Never-Ending Story

The Winchester Mystery House was built by Sarah Winchester and ended up with more than 160 rooms after she visited a psychic who told her that it must never be finished. By the time the owner died, the house had accumulated 10,000 windows, 2,000 doors, 40 staircases, and 13 bathrooms.

Lucky Sort

In the 2004 Spanish Christmas lottery, which had prizes totaling $648 million, the jackpot was shared by 195 winning tickets that were sold in the Catalan town of Sort, which means "luck" in the northeastern region's language.

SPOTLIGHT

OFFERS MORE THAN JUST THE USUAL HOT TUB. VISITORS CAN CHOOSE TO BATHE IN RED WINE,

SCALED-DOWN LIVING

Camille Allen, from Powell River, British Columbia, Canada, who learned doll-making from her husband's grandmother, creates baby dolls small enough to fit into an eggshell. The idea was born when she had some clay left over from a larger doll and formed it into a baby the size of an adult's thumb. It takes from several days to several weeks to create the tiny details such as nails and wrinkles and apply individual strands of mohair to imitate fine baby hair. Finally, the sculptures are hardened in an oven, then painted to enhance their wrinkles and creases.

GREEN TEA, COFFEE, CHOCOLATE, OR GARLIC-FLAVORED BROTH. ★ SWALLOWING A COLOR

Nano Knits

Althea Crome Merback's miniature garments are too small for normal dolls. They would fit the toys you might find in a dollhouse playroom. Althea, from Bloomington, Indiana, knits 1:144 scale outfits that can fit on a dime. Her tiny cardigans have pockets, buttons, even labels, and feature intricate patterns, including a reproduction of a Picasso painting, an ancient Grecian urn, and treasures from Tutankhamen's tomb. The "Bug-knits," as they are known, take six weeks to six months to complete and sell for hundreds of dollars. They are crafted using silk thread, or very fine cotton or wool, on needles as narrow as a hundredth of an inch. Althea makes the needles from medical-grade stainless steel wire.

1.35 inches

2 inches

Little Big Top

When Paul Tandy from Warwick, England, was given a toy big top circus for his 12th birthday, no one could have dreamed that one day it would grow into a prize-winning scale model of a touring circus. The original little circus tent has long since been replaced and trucks, animals, and over 600 hand-painted figures have been added. Using computer-controlled stage lighting and complex mechanisms, P.J. Tandy's International Circus is a working model that includes a human cannonball being fired into a net, a trapeze act swinging above the ring, and a juggler throwing hoops into the air.

CAMERA WITH A BATTERY, LIGHT SOURCE, AND A TRANSMITTER SOUNDS UNCOMFORTABLE,

DEAD WEIRD

Dog in a Log

In the 1980s, loggers cutting chestnut oaks near the Georgia-Alabama state line spotted a mummified dog in one of the logs piled up on their truck. The dog must have scrambled into the hollow tree many years earlier and become wedged there. The dry conditions and resins from the core of the tree helped to preserve the animal's body and turn it into a mummy. The loggers gave the log to the Southern Forest World Museum in Waycross. The dog was called Stuckie after the museum held a contest to name him.

Go Out in Style

A phone call requesting an airplane-shaped casket inspired traditional British coffin-makers, Vic Fearn and Co. of Nottingham, to put the fun back in funerals. Since then the demand for customized coffins has grown. A music teacher with a lifelong passion for ballet has commissioned a pink satin ballet shoe. A man who couldn't afford a yacht in life has asked to be buried in one, while another man has chosen a vintage Rolls Royce. Other unusual designs include a skateboard, a giant hot dog with mustard and onions, a corkscrew, a sports bag, a guitar, and a sled that will allow the customer to wear his skis when he is buried.

BUT IT'S AS EASY AS POPPING A PILL. CONTAINED WITHIN A CAPSULE THE SIZE OF A LARGE

Talking Tombstone

Tombstones haven't changed much over the years, but now death has gone digital. The new solar-powered Vidstone is a seven-inch LCD panel that can play a five-minute video featuring special moments from the deceased's life. The screen is covered by a solar panel, which can be flipped open by visitors, and the device has two headphone jacks.

Modern Mummies

Mortuary science students at Lynn University, Florida, are being trained in the ancient art of mummification. Graduates of the program will be able to offer preservation, body wrap, mummiform, and a sarcophagus alongside the more usual burial options.

Faces in the Floor

In 1971, Maria Gomez Pereira noticed a mark like a face on the concrete floor of her kitchen in Belmez, Spain. The family tried to clean it off without success and eventually her husband took a pickax to the floor and laid down new cement. Less than a week later the face had reappeared. Research showed that the house had been built on top of a graveyard, and excavations revealed several bodies, which were removed and given a proper burial. The kitchen floor was re-laid, but after a few weeks the face reappeared along with several others. There are claims that the faces are still appearing to this day.

HOME HELP

Camera, Action!

A tiny television has been attached to a pair of glasses, allowing the viewer to stay on top of a favorite program and keep moving. Although the TV is minuscule, it's so close to the eye that to the wearer the screen seems normal-sized. Japanese scientists have also produced a set of glasses that are a memory aid. Those specs come with a built-in camera and computer brain. First, you must video objects you might want to find in a hurry, saying the object's name aloud. Then, the camera films everything you do in the day. To find your lost items, just say the name and the display screen will play back the relevant tape.

Buddy Bot

Designed as a companion for elderly people who live alone, "ifBot" can chat, sing, and play quiz games. The robot, which costs $5,600, can recognize up to ten people from their faces or voices and can understand and respond to speech, thanks to the several million word patterns built into its software, giving it the vocabulary of a five-year-old. The 18-inch robot can also move by itself, avoid obstacles, detect steps, and take pictures and send them wirelessly via the Internet.

Sew As You Go

The Steinlauf family from Chicago specialized in making unusual bikes, including one made from an old iron bed frame and another with spikes on its tires for riding on ice. One day, Mrs. Steinlauf left her sewing machine at her husband's workshop to be repaired and the next time she saw it, it was attached to a four-seater bike.

7-14-2008

Burning Reminder

Forgetting a birthday or anniversary can land you in hot water, so an Alaskan jeweler has invented a ring that warms up to 120° F for ten seconds every hour during the 24 hours leading up to the big day. It works by converting warmth from your hand into electricity.

Shining Slippers

Miners work with lamps strapped to their heads; but midnight refrigerator raiders need headlamps on their feet. Combine a pair of slippers with a couple of bright white LEDs and you have a handsfree way to get around the house without stubbing your toe or kicking the cat. The slippers have weight-sensitive soles, so they light up only when you put them on, and a built-in timer delays LED shut-off until you are safely back in bed.

PATIENTS' WAISTS WHILE THEY GO ABOUT THEIR NORMAL DAY. THE CAMERA IS LATER EXPELLED.

4
ART and MINDS

SIZE MATTERS

First News

THE AWARD-WINNING WEEKLY NEWSPAPER FOR KIDS

8 Nov 2007

GORDON BROWN TALKS SPORT 2

ZAC EFRON INTERVIEW 14

ELEPHANTS FIGHT BACK

ELEPHANTS are getting their own back after years of cruelty by humans. It's been shown that elephants really do 'never forget' because scientists believe that angry elephants are now seeking revenge for the death of their parents.

Tiny Tabloid

You may need a magnifying glass to read this miniature newspaper. Measuring just 1.25 by 0.86 inches, this micro edition of *First News*, a British weekly newspaper for children aged seven to 14, was published on November 8, 2007.

Micro Masterpieces

British artist Willard Wigan's entire life's work could fit into a matchbox. At less than a thousandth of an inch tall, his sculptures look like specks of dust until they are placed under a microscope and magnified 500 times. While creating the Mad Hatter's Tea Party from *Alice in Wonderland*, Wigan lost almost a month's work when he accidentally inhaled Alice. Wigan uses a shard of diamond glued to an acupuncture needle to carve his figures.

Super-Sized Sunshade

At almost 52-feet wide, this huge parasol puts regular umbrellas in the shade. In fact, 295 normal-sized umbrellas could fit under its colossal canopy, which has an area of 2,088 square feet. Luckily, the 31-foot-high sunshade, weighing 1.3 tons has an electronic motor and isn't put up by hand, but it still takes six minutes to unfold.

Long Train

A bride in the Chinese city of Guangzhou needed more than 100 people to carry her train as she walked down the aisle. Her fiancé, a wedding planner, ordered the dress with a 659-foot train to celebrate the 2008 Beijing Olympic Games. The ten-foot-wide train had 208 butterfly knots and the gown, which took three months to make, weighed around 220 pounds. It took nearly five hours to arrange and photograph the dress in the Guangzhou Sunflower Garden.

LIVE AND LET DYE

Human Jigsaw

"The Enigma" has been tattooed to look like a living blue jigsaw puzzle. Born Paul Lawrence, he got his first tattoo—a dancing skeleton on his arm—at 20 years old. Since then, more than 200 tattoo artists have worked on his body, sometimes as many as 23 at a time. The star of the U.S. show Modern Primitives, he also has horn implants, reshaped ears, and large lip, ear, and body piercings.

Flesh and Blood

A man from Neath in South Wales is so fond of his family that he likes to take them with him wherever he goes. Gerwyn Isaac has turned his body into a portrait gallery and has pictures of his mother, father, brother, and even the family dog tattooed onto his back.

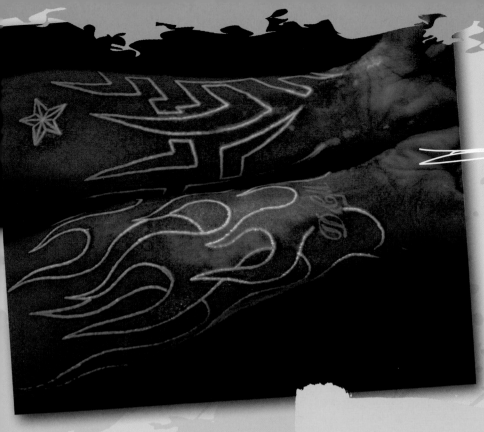

Glowing Needlecraft

Having an invisible tattoo sounds like a painful waste of time but, like a hand stamp at an amusement park, a blacklight tattoo comes to life under ultraviolet light, glowing in colors ranging from white to purple. Ultraviolet inks can be added to normal tattoos as well to make them glow in the dark.

Read My Lips

A tattoo that only a dentist might see is becoming popular around the world, often displaying a personal message that the bearer doesn't want the world to read. This tattoo trend began in the stable—thoroughbred horses are branded inside the lip to verify their identity. However, because skin cells in the mouth regenerate faster than elsewhere, the designs could fade within a year.

AIR ART

Gaty Chermaine Chu / *.98

Fan Yang has made bubbles into a theater show. He can do just about anything with them. He spins them, bounces them, fills them with smoke—oh, and he's placed an elephant inside one! Born in Vietnam, but now living in Canada, Yang once built a bubble wall 164 feet long. He can also arrange 12 bubbles within each other. In April 2008, in Perris, California, he achieved his goal of encasing an elephant in one of his fragile constructions.

As Tai the elephant stood on a specially built platform, Yang tugged on a pulley system of bubble wands that wrapped a soapy film up and around her. It was touch-and-go whether the stunt would work, as there was a slight wind and Tai seemed eager to touch the bubble. But all went well. The elephant was totally unharmed and, her owner insisted, her waving trunk showed that she had loved every part of the experience.

LEE, FROM NEW YORK, FELT THAT MOST PEOPLE WERE SO BUSY DECORATING THEIR WALLS

Float Feet

On Australia Day (January 26) 2006, 863 people with fluorescent-pink airbeds strapped to their backs trooped down to Coogee Beach in Sydney, Australia. These weren't any old airbeds though, but took the shape of giant flip-flops. It was a mark of respect for that classic Australian footwear, but also a successful attempt to line up the longest line of airbeds in Australia's warm waters. With much splashing and paddling, the participants then maneuvered the massive line of airbeds to form an outline of Australia.

Blown Off Course

It used to be the case that you went to a party and maybe came home with a balloon sausage dog or a nodding flower, but Adam Lee's balloon art is so much more. He can twist and squeak balloons into the shape of just about any body or any thing you can think of. Here the Simpsons get some air time, but this Washington state artist has also produced balloon portraits of Martha Stewart, Austin Powers, and the Statue of Liberty.

AND FLOORS, THEY WERE NEGLECTING THEIR CEILINGS. SO HE CREATED MINIATURE SCENES,

CRAFT-y WORK

Sticky Stuff

Springing up around Washington, D.C., are the translucent works of Mark Jenkins, an artist who primarily uses packing tape and plastic wrap as a medium for his sculptures. His clear, lifelike models are carefully positioned: a baby in a tree, a dog on a shoreline, and carousel horses galloping in a forest.

Something of Note

Artist Antje Kreuger held an exhibition in Berlin, Germany, that consisted of notes and messages that had been put up on trees and lampposts in her neighborhood.

Say It with Flowers

Around 150,000 roses were used in a single bouquet at a shopping mall in Frankfurt, Germany, in September 2005.

Small Considerations

For those who find a skin tattoo way too ordinary, how about these more subtle forms of body decoration: eyeball jewelry (perhaps a tiny heart on the white part) or perhaps a painting of your hero or a flag on your pearly whites as created by dentist Ron Grant.

It's the Tooth

San Francisco artist Steven J. Backman goes through more than 10,000 toothpicks a year creating his world-renowned sculptures. Using just the humble wooden device, he's made portraits of President Bush and the Mona Lisa. Perhaps his most remarkable product is an exact replica of San Francisco's Golden Gate Bridge. "It's 13 feet long and took 30,000 toothpicks, perfectly suspended, without any cable or wire," he says. "It even lights up! And took about 2½ years."

Note-Worthy

Saxophonist Aaron Bling of Jacksonville, Florida, held a single continuous low G note on his saxophone for an incredible 39 minutes 40 seconds, while standing on a New York City street in September 2007.

INCLUDING A MINI MUSICIAN'S LIVING ROOM, A SKI SLOPE, A DISASTER SCENE, AND AN ART GALLERY,

Chew Challenge

It takes approximately 40 hours and 500 sticks of pre-chewed gum to complete one of Jason Kronenwald's Gum Blonde portraits. Kronenwald dislikes chewing gum himself, so enlists a team of chewers who chew a variety of flavors and colors for him—he uses no paint or dye. He's made portraits of Britney Spears, Paris Hilton, and Brigitte Bardot.

Millions and Miles

Liza Lou of Topanga, California, used 40 million glass beads to create a kitchen and garden that was first displayed at the Kemper Museum of Contemporary Art in Kansas City in 1998. If the beads had been strung together, they would have stretched about 380 miles— the distance between Los Angeles and San Francisco.

Mechanical Art

A robot that could do origami, the ancient Japanese art of paper folding, was developed by Devin Balkom when he was a student at Carnegie Mellon University in Pittsburgh, Pennsylvania.

It's a Barbie World

As part of a promotion for Barbie, all the houses in a street in Manchester, England, were temporarily painted pink.

What Rubbish!

Leo Sewell takes just about anything he can find in dumpsters and landfills and turns it into art that sells for six-figure sums. He uses plastic, silverware, metals, and old clock parts, turning them into sculptures, collected by museums and celebrities such as Sylvester Stallone. Recently, he's had requests to recreate sculptures of people who have passed away, using their possessions.

Candy Couture

For the past 20 years, Klavdiya Lyusina, from Tsaryov, Russia, has been making accessories and clothes out of brightly colored candy wrappers— and wearing them.

FANTASTIC FIGURES

Nothing to Wear

Winner of the 2008 New Zealand Body Art Supreme Award in Auckland was Carmel McCormick, who morphed her model, Levi, into a scaly-skinned, spiky-taloned lizard. The rules? Artists could use special effects, makeup, and were awarded points for originality, design, and technique. Levi also ran away with the prize for Best Performance by a Model.

Handsome Handiwork

Artist Guido Daniele, from Milan, Italy, always needs a hand—as a canvas, that is. His mind-blowing menagerie of "handimals" includes cats, dogs, birds, fish, reptiles, an elephant, and a zebra. One animal that is out of his grasp is the rhino because hands are the wrong shape to create the horn. Each animal takes him two to ten hours to paint, using a pencil and watercolors or oil pastels. The artist prefers to use men's hands, because most women's are too delicate for some of his creatures.

KITTIWAT UNARROM COMES FROM A FAMILY OF BAKERS, WHICH INSPIRED HIM TO USE DOUGH

Spitting Image

Born in 1832, Hananuma Masakichi was a Japanese sculptor who, on learning that he had tuberculosis, decided to leave a life-sized statue of himself to the woman he loved. Using mirrors, Masakichi recreated his body from strips of wood joined so perfectly with dovetail joints, glue, and wooden pegs that no seams can be seen, even with a magnifying glass. The statue was lacquered to show muscles, bones, and veins, and Masakichi handcrafted perfect glass eyes. Finally, tiny holes were drilled to represent the pores of the skin and the artist plucked the hairs from his body and inserted them in the corresponding holes.

Nice Nails

The 3-D nail design contest, held annually in Singapore, showcases the most extraordinary nail decorations by some of Asia's most talented nail artists. The 2008 competition attracted 122 participants from ten countries, and was won by Diane Cai, who teaches at a local beauty academy. Her "queen of the forest" design included a dragon, a phoenix, a spider, a snake, and a three-headed dog, and used materials such as sand, stones, feathers, and Swarovski crystals.

TO CREATE HIS UNNERVINGLY REALISTIC SCULPTURES OF HANDS, FEET, HEADS, TORSOS, AND

CURIOUS CLOTHES

Trashy Fashion

Plastic bags, inner tubes, construction fencing, and telephone wire are the cottons, linens, silks, and wools of Seattle's Haute Trash design team. The group of performance artists creates fashion out of trash and aims to inspire others to rethink, reuse, and recycle. Chako San's wedding kimono, shown here, was made from bags and garbage from a sushi restaurant.

Heavy Steps

What material would you choose to make durable shoes? How about marble? A young man from Qingyan, China, has been wearing marble shoes weighing 143 pounds (the weight of an average woman) for the past 12 years.

Hoodie Holder

Did you know that you can dress an iPod like you would a doll? There are hats, mittens, and underwear to chose from, as well as cool streetwear.

Hoodies

OTHER BODY PARTS. ALTHOUGH HIS SHOWROOM LOOKS LIKE A CROSS BETWEEN A BUTCHER'S

Fancy Footwork

Walk as nature intended. Body artists John Maurad and Jenai Chin created these *trompe l'oeil* (French for "deceive the eye") shoes. The pair work for New York makeup agency Temptu, which specializes in airbrushing and innovative techniques. Maurad painted the details onto the feet, then Chin applied the block color using a brush. Finally Maurad used an airbrush to add the finishing touches.

Small Change

When the Hungarian National Bank withdrew its one forint (worth just over half a cent) and two forint coins from circulation at the end of February, 2008, graphic artist Tibor Gaal, also known as T-Boy, decided to make good use of the worthless silver coins. Sponsored by a glue company, he stuck them all over his suit, shirt, tie, and shoes.

SHOP AND A HORROR MOVIE, ALL HIS WORKS, DECORATED WITH RAISINS, CASHEW NUTS, AND

Mind Games

Of Strong Mind

Dominic O'Brien has overcome childhood dyslexia and Attention Deficiency Disorder (ADD) to win the World Memory Championships eight times! More than 14 years of disciplined training has helped him to correct the "imbalance" that he believes is responsible for these disorders. Along with a colleague, Dominic has used his knowledge of dyslexia and thorough research into the brain, and developed the Brainwave Conditioning System to help others suffering from dyslexia and ADD. In 2002, in front of a panel of judges, Dominic O'Brien memorized 54 packs of shuffled cards in 12 hours. He then took more than four hours to recite all 2,808 cards, with only eight errors!

Brain Power

If you measured the total length of the wiring in a Cray Computer (one of the biggest computers in the world) it would be about 60,000 miles long. Looking at the brain in the same terms, it has been estimated that it contains 200,000 miles of wiring.

No Pain, No Gain

Tim Cridland has been inspired by the mystics of the Far East. Using "mind-over-matter" philosophy, he has taught his brain not to register the feeling of pain. He can swallow swords and dance on broken glass, but it is his car feat that he counts as his greatest achievement. While lying on a bed of nails with spikes five inches long, he is able to endure the weight of a one-ton car driving over him. His skin is not even punctured.

No, this isn't a chance sighting of 007 dropping in from the skies of Manhattan, but it is an amazing piece of pavement art by street painters Edgar Mullar and Manfred Slader. They worked the illusion in Berlin's Potsdamer Platz, using just chalk.

High Expectations

Altitude can have a big effect on the brain. At 8,000 feet or higher, mountaineers have reported perceiving unseen companions, seeing another body like their own, or seeing light coming out of their body. This is probably caused by a lack of oxygen at such heights.

7 + 7 = ?
21 - 7 = ?
10 + 4 = ?
34 - 20 = ?
16 - 2 = ?
11 + 3 = ?

Quick, think of a vegetable.

(see bottom of page)

If you don't believe in the beauty of math, look at this!

1 x 8 + 1 = 9
12 x 8 + 2 = 98
123 x 8 + 3 = 987
1234 x 8 + 4 = 9876
12345 x 8 + 5 = 98765
123456 x 8 + 6 = 987654
1234567 x 8 + 7 = 9876543
12345678 x 8 + 8 = 98765432
123456789 x 8 + 9 = 987654321

CHOCOLATE, ARE COMPLETELY EDIBLE. ★ THANKS TO THE DIGITAL REVOLUTION, THE WORLD IS

Most people pick carrot. Did you?

Speed Read

Kim Peek, from Salt Lake City, Utah, reads up to eight books a day. He reads at a phenomenal rate, scanning the left page with his left eye and the right page with his right eye, and retaining 98 percent of the information.

Remember Me?

Famous memorizers in history have included Themistocles, who knew the names of the 20,000 citizens of ancient Athens, and the Roman philosopher Seneca, who could do the same for the even bigger ancient Rome. Neither, perhaps, was on a par with the 17th-century memorizer Antonio Magliabechi, who was put in charge of the 40,000 volumes in the Grand Duke of Tuscany's library in Florence, Italy, and memorized every book and its location on the shelves.

Which line is longer?

You'll be surprised to know they are both the same length.

A BIRD IN THE THE HAND

Read this phrase aloud. Now read it again.

Brain Drain

Over the course of a day, your brain uses the amount of energy contained in two large bananas, about 250 calories. That's less than a refrigerator light requires. Most of the energy the brain needs keeps the brain healthy. The added cost of thinking hard is barely noticeable.

Wildest Dreams

Dreams have often been an aid to creativity, but what mind games are at play in the following tale? The inventor of the sewing machine, Elias Howe, had been struggling for months over how to attach thread to a needle. One night, he had a dream in which he was being chased by tribesmen wielding spears. When he awoke, he remembered their spears had had a hole in them, and the rest is history!

Look at the two areas of red. Would you believe that they are exactly the same color?

Figure This

$9 \times 9 + 7 = 88$
$98 \times 9 + 6 = 888$
$987 \times 9 + 5 = 8888$
$9876 \times 9 + 4 = 88888$
$98765 \times 9 + 3 = 888888$
$987654 \times 9 + 2 = 8888888$
$9876543 \times 9 + 1 = 88888888$
$98765432 \times 9 + 0 = 888888888$

FULL OF ABANDONED TYPEWRITERS. CALIFORNIA-BASED ARTIST JEREMY MAYER CONVERTS THEM

MARVELOUS MEDIA

With two million LEGO® bricks being produced each hour, Nathan Sawaya is unlikely to run short of materials. Since 2004, the former New York lawyer has been making a living out of LEGO®, after winning a nationwide competition to become a Master Model Builder at LEGOLAND®, California. Now a freelance artist, Sawaya has a studio in Manhattan, stacked high with crates containing more than 1.5 million colored bricks. His works, which can contain up to a quarter of a million bricks apiece, include a seven-foot-long replica of the Brooklyn Bridge, a life-size Tyrannosaurus rex skeleton, a huge black-and-white self-portrait, and a tribute to the rebirth of New Orleans. Because bricks are rectangular, spherical shapes present the greatest challenge, so the globe that appeared in his 2007 exhibition was an all-round achievement. Building in LEGO® should mean that models can easily be altered if something needs adjusting, but unfortunately Sawaya had already glued the bricks of this giant hand together when he realized that the proportions of the middle section were wrong, so he had to chisel it apart.

INTO SCULPTURES RANGING FROM 18-INCH-LONG CRICKETS TO SEVEN-FOOT-TALL SKELETONS,

Cool Jewels

The gems in German-born artist Katharina Ludwig's jewelry will have disappeared by the end of the evening. Her necklaces, earrings, and rings are made of gold and silver—and ice. The idea is to contrast the warmth of the body with the coldness of ice. As the ice in the necklace melts, the chain looped inside the ice cubes gets longer. As the earrings melt, water from one collects in a little cup; the other contains pigment that leaves a mark on the shoulder. The ice gems can easily be replaced using water and an ice cube tray.

Goddess of Garbage

Most people recycle junk mail; Sandy Schimmel "upcycles" hers. In other words, she turns trash to treasure. Inspired by a stained-glass picture she saw in Venice, Italy, Schimmel decided to create her own mosaic portraits, but had trouble finding suitable materials. She started cutting up junk mail, ads, and cards, and found that the printed colors were far more varied than those of glass or tile—and the materials were free. Now the artist, who lives in Arizona, creates portraits of the famous and the not-so-famous that can sell for thousands of dollars.

WEIGHING UP TO 100 POUNDS, WITHOUT WELDING, SOLDERING, OR GLUING. IT TAKES ABOUT 40

FOOD GLORIOUS FOOD

It's a Wrap

When Joe Bravo looked at a corn tortilla, the art student saw an affordable canvas rather than a tasty taco. Now, 30 years later, the Los Angeles artist uses custom-made, oversized tortillas for his works, which sell for up to $3,200 each. Bravo bakes the tortillas first, then takes inspiration from the patterns he sees in them. His subjects have included animals, mythical creatures, and famous people such as Marilyn Monroe and Che Guevara. When the paintings are finished, the tortillas are given several coats of varnish to keep them from being eaten by bugs or animals.

Appetizing Arena

In the days leading up to Easter, the windows of specialist bakeries in the Catalonian and Valencian regions of Spain are filled with chocolate confections as pastry chefs compete to create the most impressive *mona de Pascua*. The *mona* is a traditional Easter cake, topped with chocolate eggs or figures, which is given by godparents to their godchildren. Some chefs produce amazing chocolate sculptures, including a model of Barcelona's soccer stadium using more than 1,500 pounds of chocolate and life-sized figures of sporting heroes, such as Formula One racing champion Fernando Alonso and soccer legend Ronaldo.

TYPEWRITERS AND 1,000 HOURS TO CREATE A FULL-SIZE HUMAN FIGURE. ★ "WHY BUY A

Chocol-art

Few galleries would allow visitors to lick the works of art, but British food artist Prudence Emma Staite actually encourages it. Her chocolate room, which includes a solid chocolate fireplace, chocolate paintings, lickable chocolate walls, a chocolate chandelier, and chocolate vases and logs, could feed more than 500 chocoholics. Staite's other edible exhibits include a life-sized chocolate family sitting around a full-sized dining table, a chocolate chess set, and a recreation of Andy Warhol's famous painting of Marilyn Monroe using chocolate candies.

Ap-peel-ing Artwork

Those pesky little stickers on supermarket fruit have adorned many a lunchbox, but Colorado artist Barry "Wildman" Snyder takes their decorative potential to a new level with his four-foot, mosaic-style masterpieces. Made up of more than 4,000 stickers, each takes six months to complete and can sell for up to $10,000. A handyman by day, Snyder's art evolved from placing fruit and vegetable stickers on a piece of paper on the refrigerator. Now he relies on donations from strangers to keep him supplied with the thousands of stickers he needs for his work.

COFFIN FOR JUST ONE DAY?" ASKS CASKET FURNITURE, BASED IN BRITISH COLUMBIA, CANADA.

93

OUTDOOR OUTRAGEOUS

Loco Loco

Visitors to Darlington in northern England are surprised to see a 1938 steam locomotive, complete with a plume of billowing smoke, alongside the road. However, this train is going nowhere, because it is made entirely of bricks. Designed by Scottish artist David Mach, it took a team of 34 workers 21 weeks to lay the 185,000 bricks. The train is home to time capsules donated by local schools and possibly to bats, too, because 20 special "bat bricks," which encourage bats to nest inside, have been incorporated in the hollow 15,000-ton sculpture.

Tree Cozy

How do trees keep warm in winter? Nancy Mellon and Corrine Bayraktaroglu have the answer. In 2007, they placed two pieces of knitting around a bare pear tree in Yellow Springs, Ohio. More panels were added by local residents and visitors, who included pockets and good-luck charms along with family photos, poems, and jokes. Christened the KnitKnot Tree, the ornamental pear tree wore its sweater until Arbor Day.

The Snow Queen

Having waited for nine years for someone to break their record for the tallest snowman, residents of Bethel, Maine, decided to take matters into their own hands and build his successor themselves. At ten feet taller than Angus, the original man-mountain, 122-foot snow woman Olympia had eyes made from giant wreaths, framed by eyelashes of discarded skis. Her red lips were made from painted car tires, and 27-foot-tall evergreens formed her arms. The towering giantess weighed 13,000,000 pounds and wore a red, 100-foot-long scarf.

Hairy Ride

Car shampoo has taken on a new meaning for Dutch artist Olaf Mooij since he started developing his series of "haircars" in 1999. According to Mooij, all cars have their own personalities and faces, with headlamp eyes and the grille forming a mouth— they just need hairstyles to match. Using wig fabric produced for the showbiz industry, the artist has given a classic Mini Cooper a neat gray style with a side part, while a more modern Mini received punky black spikes. Other big wigs include a ginger mullet for a Renault Clio and a samurai's topknot for a Japanese Daihatsu.

TRAILER WILL ALL TRANSFORM INTO A CUSTOM-SIZED COFFIN ON THE DAY YOU NEED IT MOST!

5

ALL SHAPES AND SIZES

UTTERLY UNIQUE

Gaeton Gets a Grip

At the age of three, Gaeton Foos from Fairport, New York, lost two fingers and a thumb in an accident. Three years later, surgeons replaced his missing thumb—with his big toe. Losing a toe doesn't affect walking or balance, but a thumb is vital, because without one it is impossible to grip anything. The surgery took ten hours, using suture thread many times finer than a human hair to connect the tiny blood vessels.

Long Lick

German schoolgirl Annika Irmler is always sticking her tongue out, but she's not being rude—just showing off her amazing asset. At more than 2¾ inches, Annika's tongue is more than ¾ inch longer than the norm. It means she can lap soda from a glass like a dog and reach the last of the ice cream inside a cone. She could even stick her tongue up her nose, but she finds the idea disgusting. So far the only time her extended tongue has caused her any problems is when it gets caught in her retainer.

★ USING ONE NOSTRIL AT A TIME, 13-YEAR-OLD ANDREW DAHL FROM BLAINE, WASHINGTON,

Coming or Going

Wang Fang of Chongqing City, China, has a job as a waitress and can run faster than her friends—even though her feet face *backward*. When she was born, doctors doubted that she would ever be able to walk, but Wang insists that the only difference between her and everyone else is that she puts her shoes on back to front.

Super Sniffer

Researchers have discovered that the reason we have two nostrils is that smelling in stereo helps us work out where a scent is coming from. This girl from Inner Mongolia must have enjoyed a better sense of smell than most of us, because she was born with an extra nostril and was able to breathe through all three. She had surgery at the age of 20 and her spare nostril has now been closed up.

It's a Fact

★ Heterochromia means having eyes of two different colors, such as one green and one blue. This is a rare condition in humans and is often inherited, but it is quite common in cats, dogs, and horses.

★ After recovering from a heart transplant, 63-year-old William Sheridan from New York suddenly developed a passion for art, and started to produce beautiful drawings. He discovered that his organ donor was a talented artist. Professor Gary Schwartz from the University of Arizona has documented 70 cases where he believes transplant recipients have inherited some of the characteristics of their donors.

★ Mehmet Yilmaz from Turkey can suck milk up through his nose and squirt it out of his left eye. After practicing for three years, using more than 26 gallons of milk, he can squirt milk a distance of 9 feet 2 inches.

DOCTOR, DOCTOR

Tool Terror

The sight of scaffolding can leave Gemma Foulds paralyzed with dread. She suffers from oikodomophobia, a Greek word meaning fear of builders. As a teenager she worried about germs in toilets, which developed into a phobia of plumbers and construction workers. Gemma washes her hands up to 60 times a day and uses a hairdryer to blow away germs in her house and car. The family from Nottinghamshire, England, had to sell their home when a building-materials store opened nearby.

Feeling Blue

Fifteen years ago, Paul Karason had fair skin and freckles. But, after developing an irritating skin condition, he decided to treat himself using colloidal silver—particles of silver suspended in liquid. Once used as an antibiotic, colloidal silver can cause a condition called argyria, which is responsible for Karason's permanent blue hue. Now known as "Papa Smurf," Karason has moved from Oregon to Madera, California, where he hopes people will be more accepting of his skin color.

A HALF PER MINUTE. ANDREW HAD TO STOP FOR A WHILE TO PUT A BAND-AID ON HIS FINGER,

True Grit

A 60-year-old man in China's Jiangxi Province claims to have cured his cancer by snacking on sand. Diagnosed with liposarcoma—a tumor in the fat cells—Sheng Shoudong started eating four spoonfuls of sand a day washed down with water, after reading about a man who had recovered from cancer by eating sand. He says he enjoys the taste and, nearly 20 years later, tests show that his tumors have shrunk.

Feeding Frenzy

Forget rubbing and scrubbing—the latest method of getting rid of crusty, flaky skin has fins. Visitors to spas across the Far East and Europe are immersing themselves in pools of doctor fish, which feed on dead areas of skin, revealing the fresh layer underneath. The toothless fish come from hot springs where little else can survive, so they have to eat whatever they can find.

AMAZING BODIES

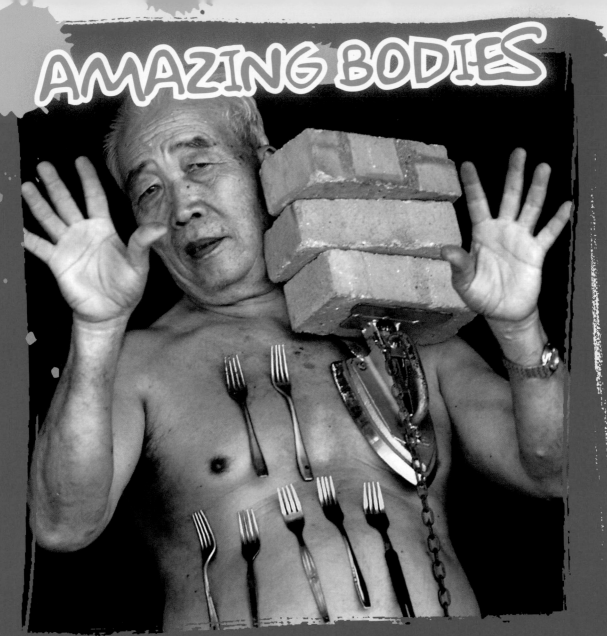

Liew Thow Lin, known as Mr. Magnet, can stick metal objects weighing up to 4½ pounds to his skin and has pulled a car 65 feet using a chain hooked to an iron plate clinging to his midriff. The retired contractor from Malaysia discovered his amazing ability ten years ago after reading about a Taiwanese family with similar powers. A medical study concluded that Lin's skin has a special suction effect, and it appears that his two sons and grandsons have inherited his rib-sticking skill. Reports of magnetic people have cropped up throughout history. Among the best known are the family of Russian factory worker Leonid Tenkaev, who found that they could make metal objects stick to their bodies a year after the 1986 Chernobyl nuclear disaster. Apparently the skill can be intensified through practice and increased concentration.

Face Furniture

A Scottish student had his face realigned using parts bought from a hardware store for less than $30, after a medical technician decided that costly surgical halo frames, normally used in reconstructive facial surgery, could be improved. Stuart Young was born with Apert Syndrome, which causes the bones of the skull to fuse together, and has undergone about 20 operations. He got sick of soup while his face was attached to the frame, but feels that the result was well worth a liquid diet for three months.

Hair to Spare?

★ You may not expect to find a food ingredient in a Chinese barbershop, but think again. Human hair is used to make L-cysteine, an additive used in bakery products, while amino acids extracted from hair were once used to make cheap soy sauce until the practice was banned by the Chinese government.

★ Barber Bill Black, from Austin, Texas, believes that hair is a renewable, protein-rich resource that should be put to better use. He has produced FertHAIRlizer®, made from human hair, and has also made a hair bikini, tie, and prayer cloth. A Croatian company has made a dress using 165 feet of hair.

★ Ronald Thompson has developed a stronger and more eco-friendly alternative to fiberglass using resin and human hair. It took 4½ pounds of hair to make the material for his "Stiletto" hair chair. Since a haircut every six weeks generates only about 0.17 ounce of hair, it would take one person 46 years to make a single chair.

★ Mats made from hair from San Francisco salons helped to clean up 58,000 gallons of fuel spilled from a container ship into San Francisco Bay.

★ A banner 80 by 13 feet at Dartmouth College was created by artist Wenda Gu using 420 pounds of hair from 42,000 haircuts.

Scuba Sensation

Mark Chenoweth, who has spent the past ten years in a wheelchair as a result of spina bifida, wanted to learn to dive but was told by doctors that it was too dangerous. Against medical advice, the Englishman signed up for a course in Minorca and, after his third dive, he discovered that he was able to stand up unaided. Three days later he was back in his wheelchair, so he booked another diving trip. He soon found that the deeper he dove, the richer the oxygen, and the longer he retained the use of his legs. The rich oxygen in deep water affects the nerve cells damaged by spina bifida and makes them work temporarily. A deep dive can keep him mobile for up to eight months.

TINY PARASITES THAT LIVE AT THE BASE OF THE EYELASHES, FEASTING ON DEAD SKIN CELLS.

WATCH OUT!

Thorny Issue

Jens Jenson, of Denmark, fell into a pile of spiky barberries in 1990 and had to visit his doctor 248 times to have a total of 32,131 thorns removed from his punctured body.

Sharp Focus

Lucky Diamond Rich from Australia likes tattoos so much that after covering his body with colorful designs from around the world, he went over them with a 100-percent body tattoo in black ink, so he could start again. Every bit of him was black, even his gums and ear canals. He then had the black decorated with white designs on top, before deciding on multicolors on the white! Altogether he's spent more than 1,000 hours in the tattoo parlor.

Ouch!

In 2007, Jin Guangying discovered why she had been suffering from headaches for 64 years. A bullet had been sitting in her brain since 1943, when she had been shot as a 13-year-old girl during the Second World War. For all those years, she suffered blinding headaches and periods of incoherent babbling. It was when her condition deteriorated that her family borrowed money for an operation, during which surgeons removed a rusty, inch-long bullet.

News Bite

Around 300 New Yorkers are bitten by rats in an average year. However, about 1,500 citizens are bitten annually by fellow New Yorkers!

Key-hole Surgery

After a joke backfired and Arthur Richardson, of North Platte, Nebraska, ended up swallowing the key to his friend's truck, a doctor X-rayed Richardson's stomach and said that the key posed no danger to his health. However, his friend still needed to use the truck. So they took the X rays to locksmith John Somers, who used the pictures to fashion a new key. Amazingly, it worked in the truck!

Heavy Meal

A 73-year-old Inuit Native American woman was hospitalized in Nome, Alaska, after an abdominal X ray revealed that her appendix contained buckshot. Doctors said the Inuit hunt so many ducks and geese for food that some of the buckshot remains in the cooked meat and is then eaten and digested.

Fine Food

Ken Edwards, from England, can eat 36 live cockroaches in one minute. When the retired pest-exterminator puts a roach in his mouth, his instinct is to crush its head with his back teeth to stop it from wriggling and scratching his digestive tract on the way down. He prefers eating the critters alive, but he says if cooked they taste like bacon.

Sharp Practice

In Sydney, Australia, Matthew Henshaw swallowed a 16-inch sword in 2005. That would be remarkable enough, except he then went on to attach a sack of potatoes weighing 44 pounds 4 ounces to the handle. He swung the sack from his mouth for five seconds.

Pulling Power

The heaviest ship ever pulled without the use of vehicles, boats, or machinery, was the Stena *Germanica*, which weighed 25,760 tons. 1,000 people from Kiel, Germany, pulled the 550-foot-long ship almost 66 feet in October 2002.

One Strike and He's Out

In 1919, Ray Caldwell, a baseball pitcher for the Cleveland Indians, was struck by lightning and knocked out, but went on to finish and win the game.

Flash Dean

Dean Ortner's trademark is "riding the lightning," in which he passes a million volts of high frequency electricity through his body. The power generated makes a wooden board he's holding in one hand burst into flames, and sends bolts of blue lightning shooting from the fingers of his other hand. He has performed this feat once a week for 30 years, yet he says he's suffered nothing more than a few burns on his fingertips. The high frequency doesn't interfere with his nervous system.

Fall Guys

Four hundred skydivers from 31 countries performed a freefall formation over Udonthani, Thailand, in 2006. The feat, performed at 24,000 feet, was to honor the Thai Royal family.

YOU CAN DO WHAT?

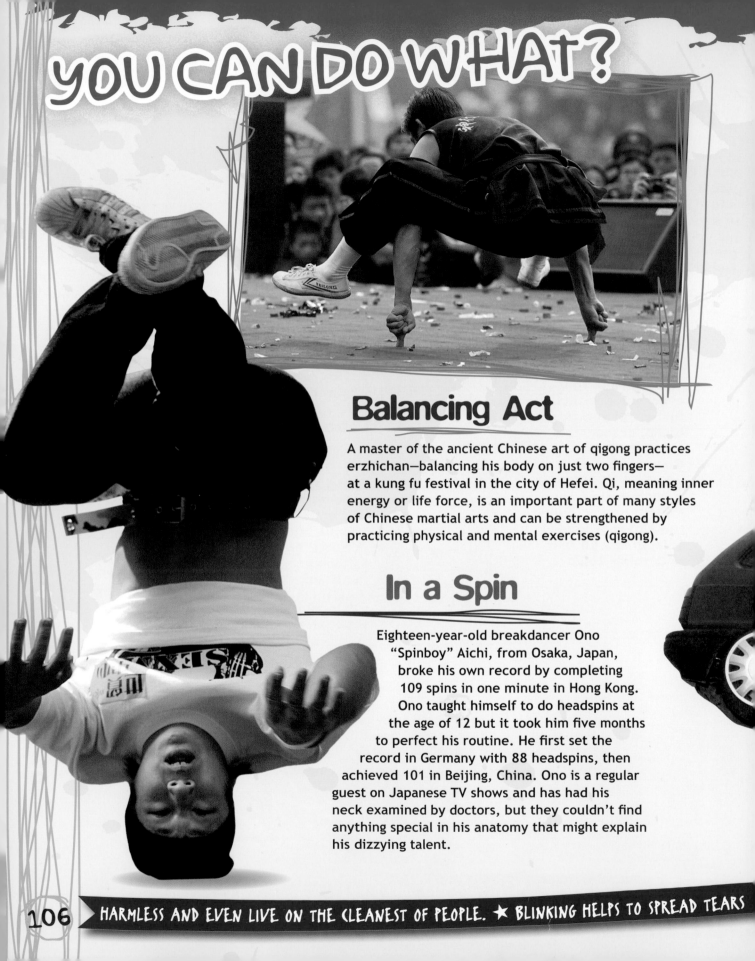

Balancing Act

A master of the ancient Chinese art of qigong practices erzhichan—balancing his body on just two fingers—at a kung fu festival in the city of Hefei. Qi, meaning inner energy or life force, is an important part of many styles of Chinese martial arts and can be strengthened by practicing physical and mental exercises (qigong).

In a Spin

Eighteen-year-old breakdancer Ono "Spinboy" Aichi, from Osaka, Japan, broke his own record by completing 109 spins in one minute in Hong Kong. Ono taught himself to do headspins at the age of 12 but it took him five months to perfect his routine. He first set the record in Germany with 88 headspins, then achieved 101 in Beijing, China. Ono is a regular guest on Japanese TV shows and has had his neck examined by doctors, but they couldn't find anything special in his anatomy that might explain his dizzying talent.

HARMLESS AND EVEN LIVE ON THE CLEANEST OF PEOPLE. ★ BLINKING HELPS TO SPREAD TEARS

Mind Over Matter

★ Eastern yogis, fakirs, and shamans are able to control their heart rate, temperature, blood pressure, and breathing by using mind power alone.

★ Akshinthala Seshu Babu from Vijaywada, India, stood completely motionless for 35 hours dressed as Mahatma Gandhi. He did not drink a drop of water, or take a bathroom break, but had to give up when his feet started to swell.

★ Zafar Gill of Pakistan lifted a 136-pound weight hanging from a clamp attached to his right ear.

Awesome Octogenarian

Xie Tianzhuang from Hefei, China, likes to keep fit during his retirement and has won more than 20 medals in the games for senior citizens. The 87-year-old can hold a stack of bricks weighing more than 77 pounds for 15 seconds using just his mouth.

Hard Head

John Evans has balanced a quad bike, 548 soccer balls, and 236 pints of beer on his head. But one of his greatest head-held challenges was a whole car weighing more than 330 pounds. The British strongman began carrying weights on his head as a building laborer, taking bricks up ladders 24 at a time. At 6½ feet tall and weighing 343 pounds, Evans's most impressive feature is his 24-inch neck.

TALENT SHOW

Number Cruncher

When autistic savant Daniel Tammet thinks about numbers they have colors, textures, and personalities. For example, number 1 is brilliant white, while 37 is lumpy. Ever since he suffered an epileptic fit at the age of three, Tammet has been obsessed with counting. He can do mind-boggling calculations with the speed of a computer and recall pi to 22,514 decimal places. Tammet, from Kent in England, speaks 11 languages—he learned Icelandic in just a week—and is creating his own language called Mänti. Yet his autism means he can't drive a car, wire an electric socket, or tell right from left.

Never Give Up

Lee Hee-ah was born with severe disabilities, including having only two fingers on each hand, no legs below the kneecaps, and mild brain damage. As a child, her mother encouraged her to learn the piano to develop some strength in her fingers so she could hold a pencil at school. Piano playing didn't come easy to the six-year-old and it took several months before she could even press any of the keys, but she persevered. Now, at the age of 20, the South Korean musician has released her first album, called "Hee-ah, a Pianist with Four Fingers."

EACH BLINK TAKES 0.3 TO 0.4 SECONDS, WHICH ADDS UP TO AN AVERAGE OF HALF AN HOUR

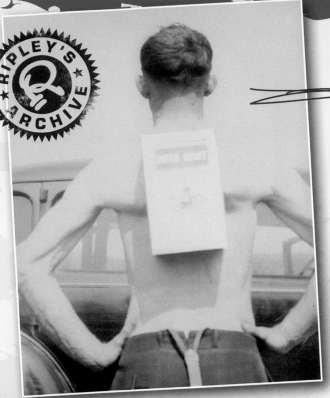

Get a Grip

In the 1940s, Joe Jirgles of Grand Rapids, Michigan, could hold a one-gallon can of varnish between his shoulder blades. He could also use his shoulder blades to attach himself so firmly to a fence that he could hang there.

Quite a Stretch

Many people can touch the floor without bending their knees, but how many can stand on a pile of books 12½ inches high and stretch over their feet to the ground below? Johnny Lucas of Stamford, Connecticut, did just that in 1935.

Toe Texter

Born in 1977 in Guangxi Province, China, Huang Yangguang lost both arms at the age of five in an accident. At school, he taught himself to write using his foot. Then he learned to paint, wash clothes, sew, weave bamboo baskets—and more recently send text messages—all with his feet. A talent contest brought him to the attention of China's Disabled Persons Performing Troupe—88 performers with hearing, visual, or physical impairments. Now he tours the world as a dancer.

A DAY. ★ CHARLES OSBORNE FROM ANTHON, IOWA, STARTED HICCUPPING IN 1922. HE DIDN'T

Creepy Tales

Burning Issue
Some people have been known to suddenly burst into flames—so-called spontaneous combustion. It has been suggested that a person's clothing and body fat can act like a candle. Another explanation is that the clothing is ignited by a discharge of static electricity. In fact, it's unlikely that the body does in fact spontaneously combust because it contains so much water. What really occurs is a mystery.

Bonjour!
When hypnotized, the famous Hollywood actor Glenn Ford recalled five previous lives. One of them was as a 17th-century French cavalry officer. During the hypnosis, Ford spoke fluent French, even though he knew only a word or two when he awoke.

Leave Well Alone
A 13-foot standing stone from the sixth century is one of a group of runestones found in Blekinge, Sweden. On it is an inscription that promises doom and destruction to anyone who breaks the monument. A local legend tells of a time the curse was tested. Long ago, a man wanted to remove the stone because he wanted more land to cultivate. He piled up wood for a fire to heat up the stone, which he was then going to crack by adding cold water. No sooner had he lit the fire than a gust of wind blew the flames at him. When the man died quickly from his burns, the fire around the rune stone inexplicably died, too.

Gone Roman
Heard about the Roman soldiers who still walk the streets of York, England? In 1953, a plumber was installing a new central heating system in the cellar of the Treasurer's House when he heard the sound of a horn in the distance. It became louder and louder, until, suddenly, a horse and rider came through the cellar wall. The rider wore a helmet and armor of the style worn by Roman soldiers. A column of Roman soldiers soon followed, dressed in green tunics and plumed helmets, carrying shields and spears. Only the soldiers' feet and part of their legs were not visible. It was discovered that the Treasurer's House was built on top of an old Roman road that was 15 inches below the basement floor. The soldiers were walking on the road, which explains why their feet and lower legs could not be seen.

House Guest
Abraham Lincoln is said to haunt the White House. Presidents Roosevelt, Truman, and Eisenhower, plus Lady Bird Johnson, all claimed to have seen his ghost.

Mmmm!

In and near the town of Taos, New Mexico, a faint, low hum is driving some residents mad. That's weird enough, but what's stranger is that only two percent of the population can hear it. Sounding like a diesel engine idling, some people hear it louder indoors. Earplugs have no impact on it. One theory is that the U.S. Navy's system of communication with submarines is to blame, but the Navy's saying nothing.

Rock in the Groove

Near Death Valley in California is a mysterious dry lake called the Devil's Race Track. Scattered around the dry lakebed are large rocks and boulders that have left traveling tracks or "scrapings." New tracks emerge regularly, though to date no one has witnessed rock movement. It's a phenomenon that has left scientists and rangers baffled for decades.

Curious Curse?

On September 30, 1955, the actor James Dean was killed when his silver Porsche 550 Spyder was struck by another vehicle. Within a year or so of this crash, the car was involved in two more fatal accidents and injured six other people.

1. The car fell on a mechanic's legs and crushed them.

2. The engine was sold to two doctors who raced against each other. One was killed, the other injured.

3. Two tires went to someone else. They both blew at the same time, sending the driver to the hospital.

4. The car was to appear in a car show, but a fire broke out, destroying every car but it.

5. The car was then loaded into a truck. The driver of the truck lost control, was thrown from the cab, and was crushed by the car when it fell from the trailer.

Light Fantastic

On March 13, 1997, between 7:30 and 10:30 p.m., thousands of people saw a series of lights in the sky over the states of Arizona and Nevada, and the Mexican state of Sonora. Now called The Phoenix Lights, the triangular formation of lights caused widespread panic. The U.S. government claimed that the lights were not UFOs but army jets. The local population remains convinced that this is a cover-up.

Bad Luck

Is this the stroke of bad luck that sank the *Titanic?* David Blair was a sailor who forgot to leave a key on board the ship. Without it, his shipmates could not open a locker in the crow's nest containing a pair of binoculars. The binoculars were to be used to look out for bad weather and obstructions—such as icebergs. Lookout Fred Fleet, who survived the disaster that claimed 1,517 lives, said that if they had had the binoculars they would have seen the iceberg and had enough time to get out of its way.

SPOTLIGHTS

YOU ARE WHAT YOU EAT

Chow Down

Colossus of competitive eating, Takeru "Tsunami" Kobayashi, from Japan took on American Joey "Jaws" Chestnut in a fast food face-off at the 2008 Singapore Food Festival. Known for his body wiggle, which helps force food down his esophagus, blue-haired Kobayashi downed 11 pounds of chicken satay in 12 minutes to defeat his rival, who managed just 8.8 pounds.

Bread, Butter, and Wine

Norma Lyon's all-butter interpretation is a first for *The Last Supper*. The sculptor from Des Moines, Iowa, carved her life-size version of Leonard da Vinci's masterpiece in 1999, softening a staggering 1,800 pounds of butter outside the cooler, before moving into the cold to complete the work. To create each figure, she applied layer upon layer of butter until a basic shape appeared, then carved the head, working down to the feet.

Food Phobia

By the age of 15, Faye Campbell from Stowmarket, England, had eaten nothing but fries washed down with milk. Doctors labeled Faye a fussy eater and suggested that she should be force-fed, but her parents were convinced that there was something physically wrong with their daughter. Specialists at a London hospital finally solved the mystery. Faye suffered from gastro-esophageal reflux, a condition where acid rises up from the stomach into the esophagus. As a child she had discovered that fries were the one food that did not cause her pain. Now on medication for the disorder, Faye is trying to widen her diet with the support of a psychologist to help her overcome her fear of other foods.

Jumping Juice

For years, frogs from Lake Titicaca, on the Bolivian-Peruvian border, have been revered as creatures with special powers. They are used in traditional medicine to treat a number of conditions ranging from tuberculosis and asthma to infertility, and their legs are a popular dish at tourist restaurants around the lake. Unfortunately, the amphibian is endangered, as thousands are illegally caught and supplied to local juicing shops, where frog juice is considered a restorative drink.

ARE SO SENSITIVE THAT THEY CAN FEEL SOMETHING MOVE JUST 25 THOUSANDTHS OF AN INCH.

Lucky Lingerie

According to one of Bolivia's New Year traditions, the color of your underwear determines your fortunes for the next year—red means you'll be lucky in love, yellow brings money, green is for prosperity, and white represents hope. Wearing underwear back to front means you are wishing for a new wardrobe. The tradition of wearing red underwear for luck probably began in medieval Spain, where red garments were forbidden because the color was linked to blood, the devil, and witchcraft. However, peasants thought red was a symbol of life, so they wore red underneath their outer clothes.

Miracle Man

When Ron Hunt felt his ladder wobble he threw the drill he was using to the ground, as he had been trained to do. But then he fell and landed face first on top of the 18-inch bit. The drill, 1½ inches in diameter, went through his eye and out the back of his head. Although his eye could not be saved, the drill bit pushed his brain to one side without damaging it, and doctors were able to unscrew it safely from his skull.

Flukes of Fortune

★ After spending $124,000 on lottery tickets over the past 20 years, Angelo and Maria Gallina probably deserved to win. The husband and wife from Belmont, California, both won the jackpot on the same day, in two separate lotteries, collecting a total of more than $17 million. The odds against the dual win were one in 24 trillion.

★ In a freak accident, six-year-old Destiny Lopez from Texas fell on a pencil, which pierced her chest and lodged in her heart. Her teacher left the pencil in place until the emergency services arrived, saving the little girl from bleeding to death.

★ Antonio Abreu Lazaga made a living as a boxer for ten years with a four-inch piece of metal lodged in his heart.

★ In 1953, a paperboy collecting payments for the month noticed that one of the nickels he had been given was particularly light. It fell to the ground and opened up revealing a miniature photograph of columns of numbers. News of the strange coin reached the police department, who turned it over to the FBI. Eventually, the trail led to Colonel Rudolf Ivanovich Abel, a Russian spy, who was arrested and tried in 1957.

Carrot Coincidence

When Caroline Scufaca of Canon City, Colorado, lost her wedding ring while gardening in 1923, she thought it was gone for good. However, 15 years later she pulled a carrot from her vegetable patch and found that it was wearing the missing ring around its middle.

Fishy Tale

When Kristy Brittain lost a nose stud while kneeboarding in rough waters off the coast of Tasmania, Australia, she never expected to see it again. Three days later, her fiancé and his friend returned from a fishing trip. She watched as they filleted their catch. Inside one fish was something that looked like a small nail—it turned out to be her missing nose stud.

IN JANUARY 1981 AND DID NOT STOP UNTIL SEPTEMBER 1983—A TOTAL OF 978 DAYS. AT FIRST SHE

115

YOU'RE KIDDING

Bobby Neel Adams is a Brooklyn-based photographic artist with an interest in the aging of the human body. In the late 1980s he began using a photomontage technique, which he called "photo-surgery," fusing together two portraits, taken in the same pose and under the same lighting. Adams does not rely on computer software to create his work, but tears the photos by hand, before joining the two halves of the different pictures together and scanning them. His project called "Age Maps" combines two photographs of the same person at different stages in their life, for example as a child and adult—the tear representing a jump in time. In a similar project, called "Family Tree," the artist spliced together two portraits of family members to form composite pictures of fathers and sons, mothers and daughters, that show the inherited features passed down through the generations. His "Couples" series shows two people in real-life relationships joined together as one.

SNEEZED EVERY SINGLE MINUTE. THEN, AS TIME WENT ON, THE FREQUENCY REDUCED TO ONCE

Tontitown Tribe

Michelle and Jim Bob Duggar like kids—so much so that they have 18, including two sets of twins. They like the letter J, too. The children's names are Josh, 20; Jana, 18; John-David, 18; Jill, 17; Jessa, 15; Jinger, 14; Joseph, 13; Josiah, 11; Joy-Anna, 11; Jeremiah, nine; Jedidiah, nine; Jason, eight; James, seven; Justin, six; Jackson, four; Johannah, three; and Jennifer, one. Baby Jordyn-Grace has just arrived. The family lives in a 7,000-square-foot home in Tontitown, in Arkansas.

Greatest Granny

In 1935, Anna Frank of Harrisburg, Ohio, had 88 living grandchildren. However, Margaret McMillan of Glasgow, Scotland, who died in 2007, had eight children, 28 grandchildren, 80 great-grandchildren and 15 great-great-grandchildren—a total of 123 grandchildren.

Good Clean Fun

Take 200 tons of topsoil and add 20,000 gallons of water for a day of fun in Westland, Michigan. Each year more than 1,000 children under age 12 get down and dirty at the town's annual Mud Day celebrations. Mud slinging is the name of the game, along with other events such as a wheelbarrow race through the mud and a contest to crown the two messiest children Mr. and Ms. Mud Day.

EVERY FIVE MINUTES. NOT SURPRISINGLY, SHE FOUND IT ALL AN EXTREMELY EXHAUSTING BUSINESS.

6

CALL OF THE WILD

TOO CLOSE FOR COMFORT

Bison Best Man

R.C. Bridges has been fascinated with buffalo all his life. In 2005, he started raising a two-month-old buffalo. Named Wildthing by his daughter, the 1,300-pound baby shares the family home and even has his own room. When Wildthing turned two, the family draped his room in ribbons and made him a birthday cake of feed and icing topped with a candle. The buffalo is such a valued member of the family that when the Bridges renewed their wedding vows, he was best man, holding the rings on his horns.

Lounge Lizards

Henry Lizardlover, who changed his name so the world would know how he felt about his pets, has more than 50 lizards of all sizes roaming freely around his Hollywood home. He started photographing them in humorous, humanlike poses—lounging on mini sofas, playing guitar, riding a bike, and on water skis. Not all the lizards are calm enough to hold a pose, but those that do can keep still for up to an hour. One of Lizardlover's favorite models, a six-foot-long, 20-pound iguana called Hasbro, even used to crawl into bed with him on chilly nights.

★ MALE CATS IN SICHUAN PROVINCE, CHINA, HAVE APPARENTLY GROWN WINGS. ACCORDING

Living with Lions

Tatyana Efremova is a trained physician and her husband, Serhiy, is a veterinarian, but they gave up their jobs to start breeding dogs and exporting and importing exotic animals. Their menagerie in Kharkiv, Ukraine, includes three playful lion cubs, who share the family's living quarters. At 18 months old, the cubs will be adult size and weigh around 450 pounds— and at this point the Efremovas will have to part with their pets.

Good Yarn

The hair in your pet brush could be keeping you warm. Victoria Pettigrew's company, VIP Fibers of Texas, spins the fur of pet dogs—as well as cats, rabbits, goats, horses, donkeys, camels, wolves, yaks, and buffalo—into yarn. It takes about a pillowcase full of hair to make enough for a sweater. The yarn is washed and treated, so that the garment doesn't smell of wet dog (or goat or yak) when it rains.

Train-Deer

Dobbey the reindeer is often spotted out with his owner, but they do not live at the North Pole—their home is in London, England. Dobbey is a common sight on the streets of Enfield, where he is a regular at the burger restaurant and the local pub—and on the train when he needs to travel farther afield. Dobbey, who lives with six female reindeer as well as emus, camels, wallabies, donkeys, sheep, and peacocks, was hand-reared by Gordon Elliott, nicknamed Dr. Dolittle.

HOW BIG?

Spot the Difference

This minuscule Vizsla puppy was born in Xuzhou, China. At 18 days old, the baby dog, seen with his normal-sized brother, was less than an inch long and weighed just over a third of an ounce.

Gentle Giant

The sight of Gibson in the front yard is enough to make any mailman tremble. Weighing in at 180 pounds, the Harlequin Great Dane is a magnificent 43 inches tall at the shoulders, but when he stands up on his hind legs, he towers over everyone at seven feet tall. He eats eight to ten cups of dry food and 2½ pounds of wet food each day, along with innumerable treats. The huge hound lives with his owner, Sandy Hall, in Sacramento, California, and regularly visits children's hospitals as a therapy dog.

Shrinking Frog

The paradoxical frog of South America is smaller as an adult than as a tadpole. Whereas the tadpole can reach a length of ten inches, the adult never exceeds three inches.

Canine Cribs

The latest must-have for the pampered pooches of the rich and famous is a custom-made pet palace. Styles can be tailored for particular breeds. For example, a French château for a poodle or a Swiss chalet for a Bernese mountain dog, complete with shutters, window boxes, and a Swiss flag. The mini-mansions are just as impressive inside, with hand-painted paw-print wallpaper, marble floors, air conditioning, and heating. Expect to pay up to $50,000 for one.

Fat Cat

The average weight for an adult cat is around ten pounds, but this tubby tom from Qingdao, China, weighs in at a whopping 33 pounds—that's more than a three-year-old child. The fleshy feline is said to eat six pounds of chicken and pork each day and measures more than 31 inches around his middle. The owner of the nine-year-old cat has to help him get into bed but insists that he is healthy.

VETERINARIANS THINK THE FLUFFY FLAPS DEVELOPED BECAUSE OF POOR GROOMING, A GENETIC

Monster Gallery

Need a Bigger Net

Passengers in airplanes flying over Lake Illiamna, which lies in the open bleak land west of Anchorage, Alaska, have described spotting 20-foot-long fish in the waters. Inuit Native Americans from the area have long told stories about these creatures, now called Illies. Fishermen also report watching Illies visit the lake's shallows in small schools.

Big Jumper

Sometimes a species throws up a giant. There's the humble frog at the bottom of our gardens, and then there's the goliath frog. Its body can be more than a foot long, and its entire length is often more than 2½ feet. It has been known to weigh more than seven pounds. Yet the eggs and tadpoles of goliath frogs are about the same size as those of any other frog. Why the adult grows so enormous, nobody knows.

True Colors

In 1924, a biologist named Le Souef claimed to have discovered a purple kangaroo in Australia. The claim was ridiculed until researchers from Macquarie University, Sydney, announced in 2001 that a wallaby with purple around its neck and on its face does in fact exist. Apparently, the purple washes off—before reappearing! The researchers think the color is secreted through the skin.

Is It a Bird?

On September 25, 2001, Mike Felice reported seeing a giant bird flying over South Greensburg, Pennsylvania. Later in November, a dog walker then reported that a creature the size of a light aircraft was flapping over the skies in Bristol, Connecticut. Journalists and scientists have since been debating whether the sightings were of Mothman, a giant birdlike creature seen around Point Pleasant, West Virginia, in 1966–1967. The case is still open.

Big Foot

Across the world are tales of the existence of giant ape-like creatures, but those about orang pendek are the most likely to be true. Hair samples brought back by a British expedition from the rainforest near Gunung Kerinci, Sumatra, did not come from any known primate in the area. Most witnesses say it stands five feet tall, walks upright, and is covered in hair. Some people even insist that they've heard it talk in a strange language.

Serpent of the Deep

Just about every three to five years there is a sighting of a huge serpent gliding through the waters of Lake Utopia, New Brunswick, Canada. The story of its existence began long ago when two Maliseet Native Americans were canoeing on the lake. The monster suddenly appeared and chased them from one end of the lake to the other. Now, locals call it "Old Ned." It is one of an unknown group of animals that travel back and forth between Lake Utopia and the Atlantic Ocean.

Hog Roasted

An 11-year-old boy tracked a 1,050-pound monster hog, measuring nine feet four inches. Jamison Stone hunted it for three hours in Alabama in 2007, before it was shot and converted into 2,800 sausages.

Anyone for a Swim?

For many years, some people claimed there was a monster called Ogopogo inhabiting the cold, deep waters of Lake Okanagan, British Columbia, Canada. It was regarded as just a legend and a bit of fun until 1926, when 20 people at the same time spotted the monster from a beach.

Pinch Me!

It's a big deal, and you probably wouldn't like to meet it, but the biggest scorpion that exists today is only one foot long. Imagine, then, a scorpion with a claw that's bigger than that. An immense 390-million-year-old fossilized claw has been found in a German quarry. It's 18 inches long, and researchers have estimated that the scorpion it belonged to would have been an astonishing eight feet long.

Monkey Man

In May 2001, reports began to circulate in New Delhi, India, of a monkey-like creature that was appearing at night to attack people. Eyewitnesses said the creature was about four feet tall, covered in thick black hair, with a metal helmet, metal claws, glowing red eyes, and three buttons on its chest. Some people insisted they were scratched, two even died as they fled to escape the attacker.

SPOTLIGHT

BUT A BRITISH SPANIEL CALLED TOBY HAS BEEN TRAINED TO SEARCH FOR BUMBLEBEE NESTS.

125

NO BRAINER

How Did It Happen?

After Mike's death, a postmortem revealed that the ax had missed the carotid artery, and a blood clot had stopped the rooster from bleeding to death. Most of the brain stem remained attached to the body and, since reflex actions are controlled by the brain stem, Mike was able to function more or less as normal.

In 1945, farmer Lloyd Olsen of Fruita, Colorado, went out with his ax to kill a chicken for supper. Like all freshly decapitated poultry, the rooster, later christened Mike, ran around for a while—but then rejoined the flock, preened, and tried to peck at the ground. Olsen decided to leave the headless chicken to its fate, but was surprised to find it alive the following morning. He thought that because the bird had such a will to live, he would feed it using an eyedropper. Mike began appearing in sideshows and was soon earning $4,500 per month (worth $50,000 today)—hardly chicken feed. Valued at $10,000, "The Headless Wonder Chicken" increased in weight from 2½ to nearly eight pounds. The end came in 1947. After 18 headless months, Mike started choking while traveling home from a tour and, because the Olsens had left their eyedropper behind, they were unable to save the valuable bird.

Chilly Chickens

When Brigitte Hawley from Kent, England, adopted four chickens from a factory farm, they were almost bald because they had been pecking at each other's feathers in the crowded shed. So she decided to knit them body warmers, which she named "chux tux." The pattern was designed to keep their wings free so they could balance, and was the winning entry in a national knitting competition.

White as Snow

Snowflake was one of a kind: an albino gorilla. He was captured in 1966 by a farmer in Equatorial Guinea, and sold to ape specialist Jordi Sabater Pi, who took him to the Barcelona Zoo. Snowflake became the zoo's most popular resident and an icon for the Spanish city. During his lifetime he fathered 22 offspring, but none of them were albino. Sadly, being white shortened his life. Like all albinos, with no pigmentation in his skin, he was vulnerable to skin cancer and died of the disease at the age of 40 (which is about 80 in human years).

TOO CLEVER BY FAR

Crafty Canines

For weeks the staff at Battersea Dogs Home in London were baffled to find that the dogs they had locked up securely the night before were running free in the morning. They asked a film company to set up cameras, and finally the culprit was revealed. A four-year-old crossbreed named Red, who had arrived a few months earlier as a malnourished stray, was unbolting his cage door, then releasing other dogs in the block. The pack then gathered in the kitchen for a midnight feast. The film was shown around the world and within a week 400 people had called to offer Red a home.

Please make sure my kennel door is always locked – I can open them!

Pigasso

Pinto is an amazingly accomplished painter—for a Yucatán miniature pig. During his spare time at Brookfield Zoo, Illinois, he creates one-off masterpieces that, during 2006, were displayed in a pig gallery at the zoo. Although pigs are supposed to be color-blind, Pinto mixes his paints with an enthusiasm worthy of any avant-garde artist—using hooves, snout, everyday objects, and even his food.

OFTEN HIDDEN UNDERGROUND AND TOBY IS HELPING RESEARCHERS TO UNDERSTAND WHY THE BEE

Rooster Ride

Chickens are not as bird-brained as they look. They can be trained to ride skateboards, play tic-tac-toe—and pull baby carriages. O.J. Plomessen of Luverne, Minnesota, was the owner of this rooster, named Golden Duke, who would pull Plomessen's baby daughter down Main Street.

Wheelies Not Walkies

Momotaro from Chiba, Japan, became a TV star when he was shown cycling to the supermarket. It took the Dalmatian just six weeks to learn how to ride the bike, which has stabilizers but has not been adapted in any other way. Momotaro must enjoy this alternative way of getting about as he wags his tail all the way.

FANTASTIC FEATS

Glide and Slide

Ever heard of a flying snake? Well, such a thing exists. The little-known U.S. Navajo flying snake has lateral winglike membranes running down its body, enabling it to glide through the air.

No Respect

Barney the Doberman pinscher was supposed to be guarding the exhibits at a teddy bear museum at Wookey Hole, England. But, during a 15-minute rampage in 2006, he inexplicably went berserk, tearing more than 100 of the toys limb from limb and causing $120,000 in damage. Among his victims was Mabel, a valuable Steiff bear that had once belonged to Elvis Presley.

Wings of Love

John Elsworth of Houston, Texas, wanted to propose to his girlfriend in a way that befitted his hobby of racing pigeons. He decided to send a pigeon bearing his words of romance. Unfortunately, the bird got lost and took his note to Rita Williams. Rita invited John over; they fell in love and got married.

Car Hijack

Members of the Leroy family of Washington discovered that a stray dog was opening their car door and climbing inside every night to sleep!

Territorial Tabby

Jack, a cat owned by Donna Dickey of West Milford, New Jersey, went into action when a black bear wandered into his yard. He chased the petrified bear up a tree and stood guard at the bottom. They stared at each other for 15 minutes, the bear clinging to the branches until it plucked up the courage to slide down. A hissing Jack immediately gave chase, forcing the bear up a second tree, where Jack remained guarding it until called away by his owner.

Light of His Life

Italian poet Dante Alighieri, who lived from 1265 to 1321, had a phobia about candlesticks, so he trained a cat to hold a candle in his paws while Dante wrote.

Watery Wallop

Marcy Poplett of Peoria, Illinois, was injured and knocked off a personal watercraft on the Illinois River after a silver carp leapt out of the water and smacked her in the face!

Home Help

When Marilyn, a Doberman pinscher, ran away from her new home in Sault Ste. Marie, Ontario, Canada, in 2002, owners Ron and Peggy Lund lured her back using a borrowed kitten. The dog adores kittens and couldn't resist its meowing.

Catty Chat

A tomcat in the Turkish town of Konya in the 1960s had the vocabulary of a one-year-old child. His owner, Eyup Mutluturk, explained that the cat became jealous of the attention being lavished on the family's grandchildren and started to speak simple words in Turkish.

Hot Dinner

Houdini, a pet Burmese python, got carried away when his owner dropped into his cage his usual food—a rabbit. Houdini had a big appetite. Not only did he eat the rabbit, but also the electric blanket used to keep the snake warm. When veterinary surgeons operated on him, they found that the reptile had not only eaten the blanket's wires, but the heating control too, which passed right through his digestive system.

Lord Lab

Jasper, a black Doberman–Labrador mix, travels by stretch limo and owns stocks worth £130,000 ($250,000). The dog, who lives with his owner, Sir Benjamin Slade, in Somerset, England, also enjoys a daily menu of sirloin steak, Dover sole, and New Zealand freshwater mussels.

Clever Canine

Bilbo, a 196-pound Newfoundland dog, is a lifeguard in Cornwall, England. He bounds into the sea to swim in front of tourists, steering them away from dangerous currents, and patrols beaches in a vest with safety messages written across it.

EATING FRENZY

Road Raider

When Arthur Boyt is hungry for a nice piece of meat, he hits the road—in the hope that something has hit his food. The retired animal lover from Cornwall, England, has been eating roadkill since he found a dead pheasant as a teenager and took it home for his mother to cook. His more unusual dishes have included owls, hedgehogs, badgers, voles, rats, cats, and a Labrador dog. Boyt insists that his truck-struck meat is natural and organic, but his wife is not so enthusiastic—she's a vegetarian.

A MONSTER TOXIC TOAD THE SIZE OF A RABBIT WAS FOUND IN OPEN LAND NEAR DARWIN,

Lucky Lab

Puppies are always eating things they shouldn't, but three-month-old Labrador retriever, Tyro, was lucky to escape with his life after swallowing a nine-inch-long knife. The hound, from British Columbia, Canada, went on to make a full recovery.

Mini Milkers

Yuri Shmakov from Ulyanovsk, Russia, is hoping to make a success of a dairy with a difference. The former civil aviation teacher will not be milking cows, or even sheep or goats. His herd is made up of far-smaller creatures: rabbits. Shmakov plans to use a scaled-down milking machine to milk the does, which each produce about a glass of creamy, high-fat milk a day.

Jaws of Death

In 1963, 23-year-old spearfishing champion Rodney Fox was defending his title in the sea off Aldinga Beach, Australia, when he was attacked by a Great White shark. Miraculously, he managed to escape from its jaws and was rescued by a boat. When his wetsuit was removed in the hospital it revealed that Rodney had been virtually bitten in half and was minutes away from death. He needed 462 stitches and still carries a memento of that day—a Great White tooth embedded in his wrist. Less than three months after the near-fatal attack, Fox was back in the water, and today he is regarded as one of the world's foremost shark experts.

AUSTRALIA. TWICE THE SIZE OF THE AVERAGE CANE TOAD, THIS TOAD WEIGHED IN AT NEARLY

IT'S A CAT'S LIFE

Reality TV went feline when ten cats, chosen from animal shelters nationwide, moved into the Meow Mix House, a specially designed mansion on Madison Avenue in New York City. Fur flew as the cat-estants competed in challenges such as the longest purr and the climb-a-thon, in an attempt to claw their way to the top prize of a job as Feline Vice President of Research and Development at Meow Mix. Each day, one cat was evicted from the house, but at least the one that got the boot was rewarded with a new home and a year's supply of cat food.

TWO POUNDS. THESE POISONOUS AMPHIBIANS WERE INTRODUCED TO AUSTRALIA FROM HAWAII IN 1935

Kitty Paddle

Cats are renowned for disliking water, but Mary Ellen Schesser was so worried about her five cats drowning in her pool that she decided to teach them to swim. The author and columnist from Oregon takes each cat into the water one by one then lets them swim back to the side and climb out to be toweled dry. They may not take a dip by choice—unless they come across a pond full of fish—but at least they know what to do if they fall in.

Circus Cats

A former clown with the Moscow State Circus, Yuri Kuklachev was inspired to start working with cats after adopting a stray kitten he found begging for food while standing on her hind legs. He founded the Moscow Cats Theater in 1990 and the troupe now has 120 feline members. Maruska is the star, performing a handstand on Kuklachev's palm, while the other cats' tricks include tightrope walking and riding a rocking horse.

Potty Training

Scooping kitty litter is no fun. At a lifetime cost of more than $3,500, it represents about half the expense of keeping a cat, so teaching your pet to use a human toilet is a great idea. The training system consists of a special toilet seat with four perforated rings, each filled with a small amount of kitty litter. As the cat gets used to using the new litter box, the rings are removed one by one, reducing the amount of litter and enlarging the opening to the toilet.

TO PREY ON SUGAR CANE BEETLES, BUT THEY HAVE NOW BECOME PESTS IN THEIR OWN RIGHT.

SOME ME TIME

Purr-fect Paradise

Animal photographer Bob Walker and his artist wife, Frances Mooney, have transformed their home into a feline fun zone for their 11 cats. Almost every room in their San Diego house has brightly colored catwalks, tunnels, and lookout stations. The high walkways lead to mousehole-shaped openings cut into the walls so that cats can move easily from room to room.

Star Paws

May the force be with you! Now true party animals can dress up as their favorite *Star Wars* characters. The idea may be barking mad, but dogs have their own range of fancy dress designs so they are not left out at Halloween or party time. The canine costumes include Yoda, Darth Vader, and Princess Leia.

THERE ARE MORE THAN 200 MILLION CANE TOADS IN AUSTRALIA, POISONING MOST NATIVE

Pampered Pets

★ Offering five-star luxury for dogs, cats, rabbits, ferrets, and hamsters, the Pet Inn Royal at Tokyo (Japan) airport has 170 rooms and suites, and charges up to $185 a night. Owners can check on their pets via a webcam while they are away.

★ Dogs will soon get their own cell phones, designed to clip on to their collars, so their owners can talk to their best friends over a two-way speaker.

★ Whether it's a pink Shirley Temple wig for a Westie, dreadlocks for a Dalmatian, or braids for a beagle, a Florida company can cater for every canine's bad hair day with a range of wigs and hair extensions.

O$_2$ 4 K9s

Inhaling pure oxygen has been an alternative therapy for humans since the 1990s. But now the service has been extended to dogs. OWND café (which stands for Oxygen, Water, Nutrition, Detox) in Tokyo, offers pets and their owners the chance to enjoy side-by-side health and beauty rejuvenation. There are 12 dogs O$_2$ capsules at the café in three sizes to accommodate small, medium, and large dogs.

ANIMALS—FROM SNAKES AND KANGAROOS TO THE SMALL CROCODILES THAT DARE TO EAT THEM.

137

FINE FIGURES

Eye-Catching Kitten

Named Cy, short for Cyclops, this kitten was born with one large eye and no nose. This rare birth defect, called cyclopia, occurs in an estimated one in 16,000 live animals. The ragdoll kitten was one of a litter of two, born in Redmond, Oregon, and its sibling was completely normal. In Greek mythology, a Cyclops was a member of a race of giants with a single eye in the middle of their foreheads.

Hopping Hound

A five-month-old dog born with no front legs has adapted well to life as a biped (two-legged creature), and jumps around like a kangaroo. The dog's mother and brother are both quite normal.

138

★ WENDY, A WHIPPET FROM CENTRAL SAANICH, CANADA, HAS A MUTATED SET OF MUSCULAR

Rare Rodent

It's enough to confuse a cat. Mice use their tails for balance, but this unusual mouse was born with two. Does that mean it is twice as agile as the average mouse?

Seeing Double

This two-faced calf was born in Lintao County, China. It has a rare condition, called diprosopus, which is thought to occur when twins start to form but don't fully separate. The calf's body is normal with one set of limbs and two ears, but it has two pairs of eyes, two mouths, and two noses.

INDEX